# Show Your Ink

*Stories About Leadership and Life*

Todd Dewett Ph.D.

ISBN: **069226194X**
ISBN 13: **9780692261941**
Library of Congress Control Number: **2014946944**
TVA Incorporated, Houston, TX

*To Cheryl—thanks for being my best friend. I am grateful for your love and support and look forward to creating many more wonderful memories. To Laura, Paxon, and Parker—thanks for giving me such a wonderful, loving, and supportive family! To all of the people who inspired these stories—thank-you for allowing me to use your experiences and our shared experiences. They have taught me a great deal. To Mom and Dad—thank-you for showing me that real transformation is possible.*

# Contents

# Introduction

They say you are not fully grown up until you lose a parent. I was there to hold my father's hand as he took his last breath. Five years later, I was privileged to do it again, this time with my mother. At thirty-eight, for better or worse, I was fully grown up. I will never forget the bravery they both showed during their final days. It lit a fire in me. The fact that life is finite became amazingly real. Once you understand this, you face a choice. You can choose to live the rest of your life in fear of how little time you have left, or you can choose to live the rest of your life fearlessly. I chose the latter. I am writing this book in honor of my mother and father and in the hopes of motivating you to make the same choice.

I began writing *Show Your Ink* with a focus on the power of being authentic. The book title was inspired by my decision to stop hiding my tattoos in professional contexts. In many ways, authenticity is every bit as powerful as competence. Through stories, I'll argue that great leadership begins by improving yourself before trying to lead and improve others. Your IQ and competence might be stellar, but they can be easily wasted if you are not as human and approachable as you are smart. In fact, I specifically discourage too much impression management. Making productive connections is about being real.

Success in life requires you to develop yourself in a manner that helps others see the complete you: the strengths *and* the imperfections, the accomplishments *and* the continued striving. At work, only when colleagues see you as human will they be open to you as a genuine leader and not merely a person occupying a position above them. I wanted *Show Your Ink* to make the case that people love—and often crave—authenticity in others.

As I began to collect my thoughts and write the stories, I realized that I wanted to share a wider array of ideas. In fact, you, my audience, forced me to do this! I would tell my stories at events, and people would come up afterward to tell me their stories and explain what they got out of my stories. What I learned is that people who want to grow and improve might see a multitude of themes where I had only seen one or two. As a result, I decided to expand my focus. So, thanks to you, I believe the book is now more useful with a broad focus on life, relationships, and success, not just authenticity.

*Show Your Ink* was originally just a phrase intended to remind us to be authentic. Over time, it became something much bigger. It's really about becoming a better version of yourself. The stories highlight a handful of classic variables known to help you achieve just that. From authenticity to sacrifice to humility to hard work, the elements of success are not a mystery. We just have to remember them and stay focused. Enjoy.

# Story 1

# Let Them See the Real You:
## *Show Your Ink*

Authenticity is an easy topic to understand, but it turns out to be a terribly difficult one to embrace. There is a battle taking place. On the one hand, there is you and your idiosyncratic desire to be expressive in life. On the other hand, there are the requirements and expectations placed upon you by the groups that surround you. These groups include work, home, school, church, and all other groups or places you frequent. The needs of these two competing systems (you and any given group) are not perfectly aligned. The result is pressure to conform to the needs of the group.

Knowing this makes you smart. Bending as necessary makes you savvy—to an extent. To help the systems around you function, it makes sense. After a certain point, however, we overindulge in meeting the needs of the groups around us. We are what we believe they need of us, but the person we supply is only a muted, half-honest version of ourselves. To some, it might seem counterintuitive, but what the systems around you really need is less conformity and a bit more authenticity.

The more others see and respect the real you, the more they will be receptive to your unique ideas and contributions. However, to deviate from expected behavioral norms is to take a risk. That's why I like to say that you have to earn the right to be authentic. You have to earn the right to be fully you. You do this through great performance. When you finally make it happen, it's amazing how many people will want to form productive relationships with you.

It all started for me when I was twenty-five years old. I was working for the world's largest consulting firm. I was young. I was hungry. I wanted to advance. To make that first promotion happen quickly, I knew I needed a big win. For some time, it eluded me. Then, finally, thanks to luck and a little clever thinking, I found it. Working with a large manufacturing client, I had fig-ured out a way to reduce a machine's changeover time from three hours to less than three minutes. This change increased the client's production capacity exponentially.

Huge win! Lots of visibility. My boss was thrilled. I could taste the promotion.

A few weeks later, I was sitting in the office, work-ing, when the telephone rang.

It was my boss. He said, "Todd, would you come to my office for a moment?"

"Sure, be right there," I replied. Wham! I set the phone down and grinned ear to ear. *Here it comes! Promotion time!* I didn't really walk down the hall. I skipped. The feeling of elation was fantastic.

I knocked on his office door, and he waved me in. "Hey, Todd," he said with a half smile. "Would you shut the door, please?"

I shut the door. *Let's do this!*

"Have a seat, please," he continued, his smile now gone. "Would you mind telling me what in the hell is on your left arm?" He pointed to my arm. His anger was palpable.

I was wearing a long-sleeved, button-down shirt with the sleeves rolled up. I pointed to the snake protruding below my sleeve. "This? That's a snake," I said nervously.

"I don't care what it is," he continued. "I do care that the client noticed. They didn't like it. They questioned how we hire people. One of them even said they thought it looked like a part of the male anatomy."

I felt like the air had been knocked out of me.

He was fuming but went on, "Listen carefully. If you want to stay at this firm, you will never again let your tattoos be seen by the client or here at work. Do you understand me?"

I faced an important moment. Stand my ground since I had done nothing wrong, or recognize the importance of managing impressions. I hesitated for only a moment. Then, I folded like a cheap suit.

"Yes, sir. Of course," I replied. "Of course."

Ten years later, I was at the back end of a career as a management professor and the front end of a career as a speaker. One day, an old friend called. Kimberly was a good buddy I knew back in high school. She was coming through town on business and suggested we get together for lunch.

The day we were scheduled to meet, I had a local speaking gig. I wore my typical uniform: khakis, a black button-down, shiny dress shoes, and a super-spiffy sports coat.

I always wore acceptable business attire. I did this in order to meet the expectations of my audiences, which were mostly corporate white-collar professionals. I even shaved regularly. I also wore professional attire in order to cover up my tattoos. I had learned my lesson from that fun incident when I was twenty-five. I didn't want to freak out more conservative audiences.

The gig that morning was fun as always. I then headed to lunch. When I walked in, I was still wearing the sports coat I had worn while speaking.

Kimberly and I hugged, sat down, and talked briefly about our children.

Then she asked, "Was it a good event this morning?"

"Awesome," I replied. "A group of accountants. Huge fun."

She looked at me carefully, smirked, and said, "Good for you. You know what? That sure is a snazzy jacket."

I thanked her, knowing she was ribbing me. I ignored the comment and ordered a beer.

She continued anyway. "Did you wear that while you were speaking?"

I nodded.

Kimberly laughed and asked, "When did you become a jacket guy? Fancy, fancy. You're not a jacket guy, Todd. You know it, and I know it."

I smiled and explained that I needed to meet the professional expectations of my audience. I told her I did not want to unnecessarily alienate people. I shared the whole story about getting busted for exposing my tattoos when I was twenty-five. I talked about why managing impressions is important. My goals, I explained, were to be safe and give people what they expect.

She laughed again and said, "You want to be an actor? I thought you wanted to be a speaker. I mean, maybe you're right. That does make you socially aware, but you know what? You're not the same guy today that you were at twenty-five. You're in a different industry, and you're far more accomplished. Plus the world has changed a lot too." She paused, and then delivered some of the best advice I've ever received. She said, "I'll bet if you take off the jacket, roll up your sleeves, and show your ink, they will like you even more. That's when they'll really start to listen. Let them see the real you."

I offered a very skeptical "Really?"

With calm conviction, she said, "Yes. Know why? Because people like real."

*People like real. Interesting,* I thought. I felt she was being honest but not necessarily accurate. I viewed her advice as intriguing but maybe a little reckless. My beer arrived, and I changed the topic.

After our lunch, I couldn't stop thinking about her comments. Over time, the more I thought about it, the more I saw the truth. Kimberly was profoundly correct. I was a tenured professor, so I felt I had the security to embrace being as authentic as I wanted to be. I decided to stop caring as much about managing impressions professionally. Life was too short for anything else.

It made me a far better speaker. I know that because the more honest and open and real I became, the more people in the audience did the same. Soon enough, people from the audience began staying after the show to share their stories. The stories they shared blew me away. I remember the association president who told me about her double mastectomy and the beautiful tattooed roses that grew on her chest. I remember the man who told me that losing one of his testicles to cancer was the best thing that ever happened to him because it taught him that life was precious.

It took me a while to become fully authentic, but I did—and so can you. Now it's your turn, so let's get started. This book is simple by design. Read each story, and then grab something to write with and start reflecting on how you can use the information in your own life. By the time you finish the last story, you'll have the rough plan you need to start working on an even better version of yourself.

# Story 2

# Using Your Mistakes: *For the Love of Ham*

Too many leaders get lost inside the status bubble. That's the invisible barrier surrounding all leaders that makes it more difficult for people beneath them to feel comfortable being honest and forthright with them. You can be a good leader and a kind person, but the status bubble still exists as a by-product of the position you occupy. The status bubble kills real conversation, turns candor into censoring, and heavily distorts the feedback leaders receive.

It also makes it difficult to deal effectively with your mistakes. The status bubble makes it easy to hide them and not talk about them. Consequently, it robs you of the chance to use your mistakes to build rapport with your team. The following is a great example of this that I encountered several years ago.

I was sitting in my office one day when the phone rang. It was the president of a company. His name was Mike. He told me he was calling to discuss some employee issues at his company, a quickly growing professional services firm specializing in human resources.

When we finally met at his office, Mike explained, "I feel like our growth has strained the employees. We feel less like a family these days. People comply, but I'm not sure they feel as committed as they once did."

As a jumping-off point for our discussion of morale and engagement, I asked him to tell me about the types of things he was doing to recognize and reward his employees.

Mike rattled off several programs the company had used in prior years. Each basically amounted to handing out trinkets from some sort of corporate catalog: coffee mugs, T-shirts, stress balls, and golf shirts. Following each effort he described, he would say, "Well, I think we did that for a few months, but I'm not sure people felt very motivated, so then we tried..."

As he was explaining what the company had done, Mike seemed to notice my disapproval. I don't hide what I'm thinking very well. I must have rolled my eyes at the thought of coffee mugs and golf shirts.

He smiled and said, "You don't seem impressed. Fair enough, but wait—there is one thing we do that everyone loves."

I replied, "Great. What's that?"

"Well," he continued, "every quarter, we have a company meeting. I get on stage and do the big tap dance—you know, revenues, margins, profits—the whole state-of-the-company speech. When I'm done, I bring up a handful of employees who have been nominated by their peers as the employees of the quarter."

I responded enthusiastically, "Nice. I've seen many versions of these ceremonies, and they can be quite effective. So, what do you give them?"

Mike sat back, relishing the moment. He paused. Then, like a proud father, he said, "I give them a ham."

My enthusiasm disappeared. I frantically suppressed my desire to giggle. I had just met this person, and I was in interview mode. The meeting turned into a nice, long coaching gig with his team, but that day, I didn't know what the outcome would be. What I did know was that it would be rude to laugh.

I composed myself and asked, "So, how's that ham thing working for you?"

He didn't miss a beat. "They love it! It's one of the few things around here that everybody really appreciates."

I had my doubts. In the following weeks, I proceeded to conduct various interviews with his employees, facilitate a few focus groups, and chat with folks by the water cooler and the picnic tables out back. I inquired about a number of topics, especially the ham scheme.

What do you think I learned about the ham scheme? The ham scheme was the biggest shared source of ridicule and condemnation in the entire organization! *Shared* is a big word in my world when you're talking about things such as teams and organizational culture. At this company, the employees didn't always agree about everything, but they sure did agree that the ham scheme was ridiculous. It had become the symbol for how disconnected management really was. Any time the employees wanted to make a joke about management, you'd better believe there was a ham involved.

The fascinating part was how utterly disconnected the president seemed to be. The status bubble can sometimes distort feedback to the point that the person lost in it is completely blind. The ham was a widely embraced joke, and yet Mike thought everyone loved and appreciated the quarterly ceremony.

Todd Dewett Ph.D.

Soon after I learned the truth about the ham, the next quarterly meeting rolled around. Hundreds of employees filled a large auditorium. I sat in the back, watching the event unfold. Mike took the stage. Customers, margins, profits! He did a great tap dance. The audience seemed interested and appreciative...until the tap dance ended.

Mike began the recognition ritual by reiterating the importance of hard work and achievement. It quickly became a nonverbal train wreck. Employees stared at their shoes, looked at their watches, rolled their eyes, and shook their heads. Mike seemed oblivious. He announced the names of that quarter's three victims. Polite applause followed, completely void of real enthusiasm. The three hapless winners took the stage.

Mike handed each one a ham, smiled, thanked them, shook their hands, and posed with them for a picture. To this day, I don't know where he got the idea that hams would make a great gift. I do know that everyone hated them. The recipients were actually the butt of the joke twice: once while on stage receiving the ham, and again when the photograph of them appeared in the company newsletter the following month.

I watched as the three unenthusiastic "winners" exited the stage. They were not smiling. The audience was uninterested. I was fascinated. I resolved then and there to learn the fate of those three hams. When the meeting was over, I quickly stalked those individuals, and I learned what became of the hams. When I did, I knew I had to do my job, so I walked into Mike's office.

"Mike, I need to tell you something," I said. Before he could speak, I realized what I really wanted to say and corrected myself. "No, I think I need to *show* you something. Would you come with me for a minute?"

He looked puzzled but agreed. He followed me out of his office, through the cubes, out the front door, and around the back of the three-story brick building that was his company. In the back sat an industrial-size dumpster. I knew that no words were necessary. I opened the huge top of the dumpster. Sitting inside were two of the three hams he had handed out.

Mike looked astonished, then appalled, then furi-ous. There he stood, in a very expensive suit, hands on the rim of this massive dumpster, trying to get a better look inside. To me, it appeared he was about to jump in to retrieve the hams. I thought I might have to restrain him. Instead of jumping in, he just turned away slowly and then began cussing. Loudly. Mike was a refined man, but pushed too hard, he could use words that would make a trucker blush.

It turns out that using expletives is something of an art form, and this man was a true artist. Mike began to rattle off a long list of off-color statements to convey his feelings. It was ugly—and kind of funny. Here is some good advice for practitioners of coaching: you can't coach extreme emotions; you can only allow them to dissipate and then engage the person rationally when he or she falls back into a normal range of emotions. So I waited.

A minute later, Mike ran out of colorful expressions and stopped to take a breath. He looked at me, exasperated, and said, "Well, what do you think I should do, Doc?"

I did what all great consultants do: I made something up right there on the fly. I said, "Here's what you do. You call a meeting. Let's make it next Tuesday at two in the afternoon. Tell everyone in the company to meet you in the parking lot in front of the building. All hands on deck—no exceptions. Be there or else, but don't tell them why; just tell them to be there. Now, when two o'clock rolls around next Tuesday and everyone is gathered in the parking lot, I want you to show up, on the roof, three stories up, looking down at them—and I want you to bring a ham."

I told him to give some version of this speech: "Hi, everyone. Can I have your attention, please? Look, I found the hams in the trash. I can't believe it took me this long to figure out that you folks don't like the hams. Frankly, I'm a little embarrassed. When I figured this out, I realized that you probably know each other better than I know you, which is why, from now on, I will not be passing out hams! I'm going to put together a cross-functional group—someone from each department—give them a little budget, and let you guys own the process of coming up with the criteria and the awards for the employee recognition program. I look forward to seeing what you come up with. No more hams!"

Of course, you can't advise a guy to get on a roof and give that speech while holding a ham without also advising him to end the speech by chucking the ham. It just seemed appropriate to me at the time. Did you know that when those hams are manufactured, they are injected with a lot of liquids? Just a side note. Anyway, I told him to do this.

He looked at me, a bit stunned, and asked, "How much am I paying you?"

I did not remind him. Instead, I started a great conversation about the need as a leader to be human, to be real, to laugh at yourself, and to make it OK for others to laugh at you too. Confidence and competence are spectacular, but so are humility and a little self-deprecation. After a small amount of arm twisting, he agreed.

The following Tuesday finally arrived. At 1:00 p.m., I was with Mike in his office, working on the speech. He was nervous. I knew this had to work, or my tenure as an advisor and coach to this organization would be over. We could hear the throngs of employees moving through the office as they began to assemble in the parking lot in front of the building.

Minutes later, I stood on the roof behind Mike and out of sight of the employees below. He looked at me and said nothing, but his facial expression screamed, "You'd better be right, pal!" I smiled and handed him the ham. He turned around and stepped closer to the edge.

The crowd of employees gasped at the sight of their leader standing on the roof of the building. The speech was short, honest, and funny. He delivered his words with sincerity and vigor. He even laughed at himself a little while speaking. He did a spectacular job of speaking from the heart.

When I had coached him earlier, I suggested it might be fun—assuming the speech went well—to end by carefully dropping the ham over the edge of the building. I thought it would be funny and symbolic of the change he was describing. However, when he saw how strong the reaction was to his speech, he got excited. He decided not to drop the ham. Instead, he reached back and threw a long Hail Mary into the middle of the hundreds of employees below.

I nearly died. I had images of someone getting knocked out, lawsuits, and so on. Thankfully, nobody was hurt by him chucking the ham with all his might. How do you think the gathered hundreds responded?

Cheers! There was a massive outpouring of shared positive emotion, the likes of which had never been seen before in the history of the company. In an instant, this man, who had fallen prey to the status bubble, now seemed real. He was three stories removed from them, but for the very first time, he didn't feel removed. He had crossed a rare leadership hurdle. He was still clearly the leader, but now he also felt like a member of the team. Mike raised his hands above his head in victory as the employees laughed right along with him.

I finally walked to the edge and looked down at the parking lot. I saw a crowd of people dancing around an awful mess of ham goo. Everyone was smiling and laughing (except the kind janitor, who knew he was going to be asked to clean up the mess).

Mike looked over at me and smiled. I smiled back, knowing my gig would continue a little longer.

At the next quarterly meeting, I once again sat in the back of the massive auditorium. Mike took the stage and began the tap dance. When he finished, he said, "As you know, there will be no hams today." People giggled and applauded. Mike then introduced the team that had been appointed to come up with the awards.

Sadly, the new team basically decided to once again hand out trinkets from a corporate catalog. I thought their decision stood no chance of motivating people. I was a little right and a little wrong. As I watched the ceremony, I recognized something. While the crowd might not have been enthralled with the gifts presented, they didn't sport the looks of disinterest and outright disgust I'd seen during the ham presentation.

I thought about it, and it made complete sense. They now owned the process. Their voices had been heard. Making fun of the trinkets being handed out would be the equivalent of making fun of themselves. After the meeting, I hung out in the cafeteria, by the smoke-break area, and out back by the picnic tables. There were no ham jokes as there had been before. Instead, I heard employees talking about how they could tweak the awards process and make it even better next time. I heard people taking ownership.

I also heard many folks making positive, supportive comments about the president. In the following days, I also saw several employees speaking to him more openly and comfortably. The status bubble had clearly sprung a bit of a leak. With one flying ham, Mike had become more approachable and real—a leader and not just a boss. He had learned to admit when he was wrong and laugh about it—and everyone loved it.

# Story 3

# Learning to Get Over Yourself:
## *A Night with the Men in Tights*

It's funny how intelligence can blind us. Don't get me wrong; IQ is wonderful, but sometimes it seduces us into lazy thinking. We stop questioning ourselves. Sometimes, we go further and project onto others by assuming they think like we think. This is partially arrogance and partially a simple reality of human psychology. In either case, it's dangerous. You need to wake up and get over yourself if you wish to truly connect with others.

No matter how high your IQ, no matter how strong your accomplishments, no matter how many accolades you've earned, sometimes you need to get down from that pedestal, close your mouth, and open your ears a bit more. Strive to see the unique individuals around you and the interesting package of traits and skills they possess. When you do, they tend to notice, and it's amazing how much more they begin to see you as interesting and worth listening to.

One of my former students, Dave, was kind enough to share a great story one night in class. The students were in the middle of a robust discussion about motivation. It was a blast. In my classroom, it was the custom to just jump in and debate. Students were encouraged to speak up and participate. Have something to say!

In the middle of a great exchange between two other students, Dave slowly raised his hand. Understand that Dave was a wonderfully atypical student. Most MBA students are in their twenties or thirties. Dave was in his forties and far more seasoned professionally than the others. An introvert by nature, he was the sole hand raiser in this particular class. When he raised his hand, everyone quieted down in anticipation because his comments were always useful and enjoyable.

I called on him. He cleared his throat and began, "I just wanted to tell the class that I agree with what you've been saying tonight, but I think it's important to note that understanding these concepts in class is one thing, while acting on them correctly in practice is far more difficult."

I nodded in agreement.

"As you all know," he continued, "I was recently promoted to my first true executive role. I've been very fortunate and have avoided any significant screw-ups or embarrassments as I've been promoted through the ranks—until now." He paused, and the other students perked up. He sighed a little, smiled, and said, "After the promotion, I started thinking about motivation and the need to say thank-you to the team for their hard work and accomplishments. I wanted to find just the right time to show my gratitude as their new leader." Dave's new role put him in charge of twenty "code jockeys"— his phrase, not mine. His direct reports were all managers of different teams charged with various types of software programing. He joked that he was now king of the geeks.

He continued, "After the first few months had passed and a number of legit small wins had begun to pile up, I knew it was time. I called the team together on a Thursday afternoon for a quick huddle right there in the middle of the office. It was not scheduled, so everyone was curious. I told them what fun it was to be the new chief of this crew. I told them that the progress they were making on various projects was impressive. I thanked them for their hard work and told them I really wanted to show them how much I appreciated their contributions. I announced that following the close of business on Friday, I was taking the whole group...to happy hour!" He asked my class, "How many people on my team do you think showed up?"

One kid piped up, "All of them—it's free booze!" Everyone laughed.

"Not quite," Dave replied. "Only half of the team showed up. I didn't understand why, and I was a little mad at first. As the night wound down, I found myself talking to the one member of the team with whom I had worked in the past. This was a person I trusted and who knew me well. A confidant. I admitted that happy hour did not work out the way I had intended. The feedback he game me was surprising, but then blatantly obvious."

His friend said, "Here's the thing, Dave. Not everyone likes to drink. Not everyone likes to socialize at bars. Further, I know for a fact that at least half of the group who did show up didn't come out tonight to share a few drinks with the boss. They came out because they feared losing points with you back in the office if they didn't show up."

Dave continued speaking to the class. "Wow. I had inadvertently created a negative outcome when all I really wanted to do was something positive. It was tough, but it was good feedback. For the first time in as long as I could remember, I felt a small bit embarrassed by one of my professional decisions. When I got back to the office the next week, I didn't look folks in the eyes as I normally would. I spent some time thinking about how I could say thank-you more effectively. I wanted to get it so right the next time I did something similar that they wouldn't even remember the little happy-hour incident."

"Eventually, the idea came to me," Dave said. "This was going to be brilliant. A few months later, following a few more successful performance milestones, I found another great opportunity to say thank-you to the team. I walked out in the middle of the cubes and offices and shouted for everyone to come join me for a huddle. They gathered around, a few heads hanging. No doubt more than one thought, *Great, here comes another happy hour!*"

Dave said to his team, "Your work continues to be impressive. I really do appreciate the effort you're giving. I'd like to show you how much I value your efforts and contributions. That's why I intend to take the whole team...canoeing!"

The classroom burst into laughter. As did I.

Dave laughed with us and then said, "I actually did that." He shook his head. "Almost to a person, the same half who went to happy hour joined me for the canoeing trip. Looking back on it, they must have been scratching their heads and thinking, *Now he wants us to give up a weekend and get sunburned together?*"

"Following our day on the river, predictably," Dave admitted, "I received very similar feedback from my friend on the team. People didn't really show up to have fun as much as they did because they felt obligated to show up. Realizing that I had basically done the same thing twice, though now on a much grander scale, I felt stupid. The first time, I wasted a couple hours. This time, I wasted a weekend. I'd never questioned my people skills in the past, but now I felt like an idiot. How could they trust me if I seemed so aloof and out of touch?"

Dave said he went back to the office, once again unable to look the team in the eyes. Days later, when he started to gain back his confidence, he noticed something new. He sat in the office, just staring at the team while they all worked. He just watched them operate in their natural habitat. Then it hit him. An epiphany. A breakthrough.

He confessed to my class, "I realized the obvious. Up until then, I had merely been projecting me onto them. I was assuming they liked what I liked. Huge mistake." He paused and then grinned, "I like to drink. I like to canoe. Sometimes I like to drink while I'm canoeing." Everyone chuckled.

"My breakthrough," he continued, "was in understanding that my interests had nothing at all to do with their interests. I had to get over myself, stop thinking about what I wanted, and try to see them as unique individuals. When I realized this and started looking closely at them, I noticed something. It was right there in front of me the whole time, and I had failed to see it. I noticed that every member of the team, in their workspace, had a very clear indication that they were a huge fan—of professional wrestling!"

He described the scene. "One guy had a bobblehead, the next a poster, the next a figurine. Two guys had mouse pads with professional wrestlers on them, and several had signed photographs. It was right there in plain sight the whole time."

Dave was something of an intellectual. He told the class that he thought professional wrestling was about the stupidest thing mankind had ever created. He also, thankfully, now understood that his view of professional wrestling didn't matter. What did matter was that the team shared this interest.

Dave said, "Months later, when the team had once again completed several significant milestones and were deserving of a sincere thank-you, for the third time during my tenure as their new boss, I walked out into the middle of the office and called a huddle. I could see the concern on their faces as they gathered around. I think they were worried I was going to ask them to go skydiving or something. I told them thank-you for all of their hard work and quickly pulled out tickets to the freak show. I invited the whole team to join me the following month at the local coliseum to see the men in tights do their thing at the wrestling show."

Laughter erupted at the thought of a team retreat to see a professional wrestling show. Dave asked, "This time, what percentage of the team do you think showed up? That's right, one hundred percent. Not only did they show up, but they smiled and laughed comfortably. They looked me in the eye more than usual. They called me by my first name and punched me on the arm as if I was one of the guys. I've never had so much fun being out of my element and laughing at myself as I did that night. I could tell by the way they acted I was clearly still the boss, but now I also felt like part of the team." Dave paused. "Thank God I learned to get over myself."

Dave described how the team's chemistry seemed to shift when they got back to the office the following week. He had figured out that sometimes leadership requires you to get over yourself. Sometimes, showing your ink is about sharing something new about yourself; other times, it's about seeing something new and unique in others while laughing at yourself. When people know you're capable of appreciating the real them, it's funny how much more they become interested in listening to and helping you.

# Story 4

# Eating Humble Pie: *Real Friends Know When to Smack You*

It's funny. In many ways, our society begs you to put your best foot forward, to be aggressive and self-promoting to the point of being self-aggrandizing. Projecting strength is everything! Not quite. Humility makes you honest. It makes you human. It makes you real. You must understand that appropriate use of humility does not detract from your strengths and accomplishments. It amplifies them. False modesty is ridiculous, but a little bit of honest public humility is golden. The very best leaders—dare I say, the very best *people*—are a beautiful mix of awesome accomplishments and sincere humility.

Do you know what's even better than understanding the power and necessity of humility? Having a friend around who will smack you when you when you forget these things.

As a professor, I had a healthy ego. Most professionals do, but professors are particularly bad. They become self-deluded, believing in their own righteousness. Humility often escapes them. I fell prey to this as much as anyone. I was tenured quickly, won a bunch of awards, and was very popular with students. My head was swollen more than most.

Then, to make things worse, I began a career as a professional speaker. Look at me! Listen to me! It's a truly amazing vocation, but you have to keep your ego in check. I know that now, but it took some time. Speaking started as a fun side project for me but quickly became a serious endeavor. My head continued growing. It is vitally important you believe in yourself, but you can take that too far. A few years ago, I did just that.

I was at the Philadelphia International Airport, waiting for a flight home after a speaking gig. I was sitting alone, reading a novel.

A man approached. "Dr. Dewett?"

I looked up and replied, "Yes?"

"I just wanted to say hello. I saw you speak once and really enjoy what you do," the man offered. He shook my hand and smiled warmly.

I smiled back. On the outside, I was completely calm and cool. I thanked him for being kind and told him that I appreciated his support. We chatted for maybe a minute before we wished each other well, and he walked away. I had been collected and polished on the outside, but on the inside, it was a different story. That man couldn't have known this, but he was the very first person to recognize me in public—you know, as if I was a *someone*. I was blown away! I felt like a somebody—hell, I felt like a celebrity. To this day, I've been spotted like that exactly twice, but that day, when it first happened, I was a king! My head swelled even more.

Two days later, I was back at home, grocery shopping with my oldest son, Paxon. As we cruised through the produce section, a woman approached and said, "Hi, Dr. Dewett. I just have to say, I love your radio show! Keep it up!" She shook my hand and was gone.

Paxon knew I had a radio show, but he never thought much about it until then. He said, "Did you know that lady?"

"No," I replied.

"Wow," he gushed. He thought his daddy was special. The swelling accelerated. It was becoming a burden to carry around such a ridiculously overinflated melon.

The next day, I was quoted in the *New York Times*. My legs began to buckle under the weight of my ginormous noggin.

A few days later, I had lunch with one of my favorite cousins. We grew up together, knew each other very well, and knew all of the stupid things we had done as kids. Sarah was passing through town on business, and we were able to schedule lunch and catch up. I hadn't seen her in several years, and I was excited to reconnect.

After exchanging stories about our families, Sarah asked me about my little side business. "So how's it going with all that Dr. Dewett stuff you've been working on? I saw online that you've been speaking a lot. That right?"

I gushed excitedly, "It's been crazy." I rapidly told her about several recent gigs, the fact that I was now flying around to speak in different places, that I had been spotted in the airport and then in the grocery store, that I had quotes in the national press—blah, blah, blah!

I was in the middle of a seriously overindulgent response to her question when Sarah grimaced just a little and held up both hands as if to say, "You can stop now." If you knew Sarah like I do, you would know that she's soft-spoken and not the type to do anything confrontational. So I knew that holding up her hands in that manner was a very strong signal.

"What?" I asked.

"Look, I think it's really cool what you're working on, Todd," she began, "but you gotta remember to keep both feet firmly on the ground. I know who you are. I know who you were back in the day. I've seen you eat mud. I've seen you get busted by your mother when you flushed three-bean salad down the toilet at Thanksgiving. I was there the day your pants fell down when you were eleven while you were running the football in the peewee league." She grinned and leaned forward. "All your new stuff is great, but don't let yourself believe too much of the hype. OK?"

I nodded.

She glared at me, apparently not convinced I had heard the message. She continued, "I mean, it's great that you went to college forever and wrote a book. Woohoo! But don't you forget, you're also the kid who took a dare in the third grade to eat a—"

"OK!" I interrupted. "Point taken. Now can you keep it down, please?"

"I still can't believe you kiss your mother with that mouth," she giggled.

She was mostly serious and a little funny and entirely correct. As she delivered the message, I could feel the air slowly seeping out of my head. It only hurt for a split second. Then, it felt like a great relief. We laughed it off and had a spectacular lunch. I picked up the tab even though she tried to stop me. I bought her lunch, but she'd done something far more amazing for me. She gave me much-needed perspective. She gave me a swift kick in the pants. She used only a few words, but she effectively reminded me to lighten up and remember to laugh at myself.

No matter what your personality type, I encourage you to view humility as a skill. Skills are things we can learn. You can also boost your odds of embracing a little humility by putting the right people around you. I now make a point to stay in touch with my cousin Sarah regularly. Your turn: try to name at least one person with whom you should interact less because they only feed your ego. Now name one person with whom you should interact more because they keep you grounded. Thanks, cuz!

# Story 5

# Defining Clear Values: *That Strip Club in Mexico*

Years ago, I had the opportunity to work for a very large, well-respected management consulting firm. Very early in my tenure there, I learned a terribly important lesson: gray area exists, and you should be prepared to deal with it.

Gray area refers to that time in a professional context when you find yourself needing to make a decision, but somehow knowing right from wrong isn't as easy as you wish it was. For better or worse, professional life is full of gray area. Add to this reality the fact that we don't often have as much clarity about our personal values as we should have, and it becomes obvious that sometimes we hesitate too much and other times we flat-out make bad decisions. This, of course, brings me to a story about a strip club in Mexico.

One of my first clients was a large manufacturer. Some partner at my firm had convinced some executives at the client firm to hire us. The client, however, was smart. They basically told us to prove we were smart by having us complete a pilot project. They offered up a small part of one manufacturing facility, paid us a few hundred thousand bucks, and set us loose. If we could prove ourselves on the pilot project, we had great odds of being hired for a much larger project worth a few million.

The bad news: the client facility was located in Matamoras, Mexico. This was decidedly not a vacation destination. You might recall Ross Perot, the legendary businessman and political contender, referencing the great sucking sound that would follow the passage of the North American Free Trade Act. Many jobs did in fact move south of the border, and our client was in that group. The downside of this otherwise great opportunity was that working in the maquiladoras was pretty horrible. The local labor pool was very poor. Good people lived and worked in horrendous conditions.

Somehow, I was selected to be on the merry team of six people dispatched to Matamoros. We quickly put our heads down and got to work. Outside the factory, conditions were grim, but inside the factory was a dream opportunity—a possible career changer. Most of the team was young, and we knew what this represented. If we were successful with the pilot engagement and our firm then sold a big gig worth millions, we'd all be little superstars. Many partners in the firm would know our name. Our networks would be expanded greatly. We would have our pick of future clients. The opportunity was significant enough to help us ignore the conditions in Matamoros and focus instead on our work.

The work involved long hours, lots of time on the shop floor of this manufacturing facility, and even more hours in front of our laptops, crunching numbers and exploring possibilities. About seven weeks into our work, we'd begun making a lot of progress. One afternoon, we were all sitting in the office area, huddled around our laptops, when the plant manager—our main daily client contact—came running into our work area. He was grinning and waving a bunch of papers.

He said, "I don't fully understand every last thing you guys are doing, but whatever it is, keep doing it." He then ran through a bunch of metrics concerning the manufacturing lines we had been fiddling with. Scrap was down, throughput was up, quality was up, and so on. Everything we set out to achieve was starting to transpire, and the client was thrilled—so much so that he then said something surprising. "We need to celebrate! These are big milestones. This project is going to be a success." Then in a more hushed tone, he added, "You guys have a great shot at getting hired for a much bigger project, and I might even get a promotion since I pushed to bring you in." Back in his normal voice, he said, "We're going out tonight. You six and my management team. Go home, clean up, and meet us back here at six o'clock."

It was only two in the afternoon when he made this announcement. The client never tells you to leave early. My boss on the project never let us off early. He also knew how significant this opportunity was and how exuberant the client was. He stated excitedly, "Pack it up, gang. Time to go!"

We took off across the border to Brownsville, Texas, where we were staying. After showering and changing clothes, eventually we crossed over once more. At just past six in the evening, we arrived as instructed in the parking lot of the client facility. There waiting on us was a nice-size, white party bus. Ever been on a party bus? Vegas rules applied, I imagined. *What happens on the bus stays on the bus.* All kidding aside, we were stoked. It didn't matter where we were going. The client was happy, so we were happy.

There were fourteen of us on the bus that afternoon: six of us, eight of them. Sitting in the back of the bus as we pulled out of the parking lot, I was under the impression we were headed to a restaurant. Then I heard my boss at the front of the bus. He said to the lead client manager, "So, where are we going?"

The client replied, "My brother's place."

"What's your brother do?" came the reply.

With no hesitation, the client answered, "He owns a strip club downtown."

Silence filled the bus. Apparently, the client management team was used to this situation. They all casually looked around to check our reactions.

I was not thrilled with the announcement, but honestly, I wasn't sure how to feel about it. I was young. I was not used to dealing with the gray area. I had not spent sufficient time thinking about what it was I truly valued in life. As a result, I didn't know how to react. I wanted guidance. So I looked to the front of the small bus to see how my boss was reacting. He was a decent enough fellow. I figured I would just follow his lead.

How he felt about the situation was readily apparent. He started grinning like an idiot and began counting his one-dollar bills.

Seated next to me was Paul. He and I were the two lowest-ranking people on the team. Paul was my roommate at our corporate apartment in Brownsville. I had gotten to know him well. He was quite introverted, which turned out to be a great compliment to my ridiculously extroverted personality. We worked very well together. Paul was also a devout Christian. That was his faith, and he wore it well.

When it was announced that we were en route to a strip club, Paul nearly had a heart attack. Have you ever had someone look at you, say nothing, but nonetheless speak volumes with their eyes? He looked at me with an expression I'll never forget. He seemed to be asking me to do something. He said nothing but reeked of fear and discomfort. His eyes were screaming, *Don't make me go! Do something! Get me out of this!*

I simply said, "Don't worry. We'll be OK. We're just going to roll with it." You see, if you lack values clarity, the standard response is to just roll with it. Look at what others are doing, and just go with the flow. Not a terribly impressive response, but it's common. Things then might work out OK, or things might be horrible. In either case, it's not because your plan worked or failed. It's because you decided not to decide (always a bad decision) and just rolled the dice.

Paul sat next to me, looking despondent. Then he began to sweat. I quickly realized there are actually levels of sweating. Level one is largely contained inside your clothing. No one is the wiser. The stress level is moderate. At level two, the sweat is clearly showing on the outside of your clothing. People can see that you're melting. The stress is nearly unbearable. Paul hit level two in about twenty seconds. He looked at me, hurt, as if I had failed to help him in this situation.

I wasn't sure what to do. I simply repeated, "We're OK. We'll just roll with this."

Before I go on, let me ask you a question. What would you do? Be honest. Would you somehow try to get off the bus? I don't care about your rationale. I can support that position. Or would you choose to stay on the bus and enjoy the debauchery? I can support that position as well.

I'm not one to judge. I just want you to remember that all decisions have consequences. If you succeed in getting off the bus, you could upset your colleagues, your boss, and the client. Ultimately, this move might jeopardize the project. Should you choose to stay on the bus, who knows what types of regrets might pile up over the course of the evening.

I rolled with it. We proceeded to the strip club—a place that I'll not describe. Let's just say that the client team and my team were (almost) all having the time of their lives. I saw a new side of my boss that really surprised me. I'm pretty sure his exuberant participation was genuine, not something he simply did to please the client.

I sat next to Paul, watching the madness unfold. After a minute or two, I looked at him. His head was down. He just stared at the ground. I then realized there is a level three to sweating, and it looked like it might be a serious medical condition. The poor kid was soaked.

I was also uncomfortable. Not like Paul, but nonetheless, this didn't feel acceptable or correct to me. We had been sitting there for maybe ten minutes when I reached my limit. I jumped up and announced to Paul, "I'm going outside to have a cigarette. Care to join me?"

He jumped to his feet with a passion you wouldn't believe and said, "I'd love a smoke!"

Neither of us smoked. We just needed an excuse to get out of that place. We quietly excused ourselves and casually walked around the streets of downtown Matamoros. We talked about family, our careers, and how absurd it was that we unexpectedly found ourselves in a strip club. It was a great walk. Two hours later, the team exited and found us waiting by the party bus.

In the days that followed, it did not appear we had caused ourselves any trouble. Our boss and the team didn't talk about it. Paul and I figured they knew we had bailed but didn't really care. They knew they were not in any trouble since we had technically participated in the outing too, though we just got our fill early and stepped out. The client didn't seem to care, either, although over the remaining months of the project, we had cause for several more celebrations, and they were all at restaurants. Paul and I liked to think we had influenced that decision.

Let me state the obvious—while I do a lot of preaching, I'm no preacher. I'm not telling you what is right or wrong in this situation per se. My job is to wake you up and remind you that decisions have consequences. I want you to think about them *before* making key decisions, not after.

So here's your call to action. Take five minutes and see if you can list your most deeply held values. People value all kinds of things, from religion to family to money. In no particular order, write them down. Now. I'll wait. OK, now look at the list and realize that you can't really value everything equally. You need to prioritize. So I want you to look at your list and rank your values, starting with number one being the most important. Now take your little list and put it somewhere you can access it easily on occasion. It should become one of your key reference points for any big decision you make, business or otherwise.

It's simple in the end. Define your values and embrace them, or there's no telling what kind of harebrained decisions you might make. If you're not careful, you might end up in a strip club in Mexico.

# Story 6

# Injecting Needed Positivity:
## *The Downside of Emotional Intelligence*

In the last twenty years, the idea of emotional intelligence (EI) has gained great popularity. This is a good thing. To crudely summarize the idea, people can learn to recognize, in themselves and others, emotions as they arise such that they can effectively choose how to use them instead of merely being subject to them.

My observation of this area of thinking in practice is that two things have been accomplished. The first is very good. Our average level of emotional intelligence has in fact increased at work. Exactly how much is something we might debate, but the trend is in the right direction, and that is spectacular.

My other observation, however, is not so good. I've talked to many professionals about EI, and the vast majority tend to think only of managing negative emotions. While that's hugely important, it may have inadvertently created a weaker focus on the role of positive emotions at work. To some this will be heresy; fine, but in some ways I feel that EI has unwittingly reinforced the perception that to be "professional" is to be "unemotional."

I like to remind people that positive emotions are truly the secret sauce at work in terms of building real bonds, strong relationships, loyalty, commitment, and, ultimately, productivity. Yet, our tendency is to censor them and present a muted and measured version of ourselves. It's a type of impression management that often goes so far that we rarely experience a full range of positive emotions at work.

I learned that lesson in an interesting way. I was sitting in my office at Wright State University one summer, preparing to teach a summer school class, when the phone rang. It was my mother. Have you ever picked up the phone, recognized the person's voice, and also recognized that something was off? I noticed that immediately.

The conversation was odd. Mom and I aren't given to small talk, yet she was talking about the weather and other mundane topics. I allowed her to get away with it for a few minutes, and then I had to call her out. I said, "Mom, are you OK? You seem distracted, or maybe you're just beating around the bush."

She hesitated.

"Mom, I'm headed to class in a few minutes. Spit it out. What's on your mind?" I pleaded.

"Well," she replied, "I didn't really know what to say."

"About what?"

"Well, I just thought I'd let it work itself out," she said.

"Let what work itself out?"

She cleared her throat and continued, "I have a lump on my neck."

"How long have you had it?" I asked.

"About two months."

"OK. How big is it?" I asked.

"Oh, I don't know. About the size of a baseball."

I gasped. "Mom, why didn't you tell me sooner?"

"You're busy, sweetie. I didn't want to bother you," she replied. "But don't worry, I have a strategy."

"So what's your strategy?" I asked.

"Well, I've been praying about it every day," she explained.

Wow. I needed to know the reality of the situation. I told Mom not to worry and that I'd call her in just a few minutes. We hung up, and I immediately called her neighbor because unlike my mother, she owned a phone with a camera. I asked the neighbor to run over immediately and take a good picture of my mother. I needed to see the headshot. She agreed. Five minutes later, I received an image on my phone of my mother grinning like an idiot with a baseball-size lump hanging off the left side of her throat.

I called her back. I told her that her strategy was fine by me, though I suggested we should expand it to include medical doctors. She agreed. When we finally hung up, I looked at the clock on my office wall. I had three minutes to get to class. I felt spent, but the show must go on. No time to prep. I figured I'd just run over to the next building and do my very best ad lib.

When I walked through the door of the classroom that day, I did something I never do. I decided I would not begin the class with our usual social banter. I always started class with informal chit-chat. I would tell my students what was happening in my life, and they would tell me what was happening in theirs. It was fun, it was informative, and it eased us into discussing the day's materials.

Not this time. I just said hello, put my backpack down, and began teaching. The class looked surprised, almost startled by my formality. It became quite clear within a few minutes that the students could tell something was wrong. I tried to march forward with my comments, but their faces persisted. They were pleading with me nonverbally to address whatever it was that was bothering me.

Finally, one brave student asked, "Professor, what's wrong? Are you OK?"

I stopped in my tracks. I paused to think about how to respond. Then, something happened to me that had never happened before in a professional context. I began to cry uncontrollably. I hung my head and bawled. We've all been in that place where you literally don't feel able to stop crying. I had been there a few times, but never at work or in a professional role.

I couldn't stop. It was bad—many tears, those big awkward breaths you take when sobbing, and a lot of snot. It felt like it lasted for an hour, though it was more likely only a minute. At some point, I was able to get control of my emotions, realize what I was doing—and where—and begin to turn off the faucet. I took one last huge sniff, ran my hand under my nose, and raised my head back up.

What I saw surprised me and moved me. I saw a room full of MBA students crying. I didn't know what to do. I felt like a failure. I felt like I had no emotional intelligence. I felt like I had just modeled an embarrassing lack of control in front of my students. I don't enjoy feeling out of control, and I certainly don't enjoy feeling like a failure.

So, I did the only thing in that moment that seemed reasonable. I acted like the entire scene had not happened. I wiped my eyes quickly, opened my mouth, and jumped into a lecture. It never happened!

The students were more shocked by my refusal to address the breakdown than they were by the breakdown itself. I droned on as I am wired to do, preaching endlessly about aspects of leadership and life. I zealously ignored their pleading eyes. They were dying for me to stop and just talk to them. They wanted to hear more. They wanted to offer me support. I would have nothing to do with it. I erased that little moment of weakness from existence.

I pushed through my class material and then surprised the students once more. When class ends, I normally stick around and chat with them. Not that night. I wrapped up my last point, thanked them, grabbed my stuff, and headed out the door. The odd night was over and soon to be forgotten.

Mom lasted about two months after that phone call. A surprisingly good two months. I spent nearly all of it with her, caring for her, laughing with her. My father had already passed, so it was just her and me. And then she was gone.

Two years later, I was on stage in St. Louis, telling stories to a room full of more than one thousand people in a huge auditorium. The gig was going well. People were laughing and learning. Then, I got to a story about my father. It's a great story about why one should always strive to adopt a positive perspective.

It's also a tough story because it involves my father's battle with cancer. Whenever others hear a story about someone fighting cancer, it inevitably brings to mind the thoughts and emotions they felt when someone they knew was dealing with the disease. I'd seen this happen many times with this story. I start to speak, people can relate, and then someone starts crying.

In St. Louis that day, there was a woman sitting off to the right side of the stage in a blue suit. I dived into the story, she tuned in—simultaneously listening to me and also no doubt thinking about someone she loved and that person's journey with cancer. She began to cry. Within twenty seconds, the woman sitting next to her began to cry.

If there's one thing we know for sure about emotions, it's that they are contagious. When one person in a large group begins to cry, others will join in. It moves like a virus snaking through the group. I've been on stage many times and watched that emotional vibe jump around the audience as I shared the story about my father.

It started with the woman in the blue suit. Then, something new happened that day in St. Louis. The vibe jumped up on stage and smacked me. I could feel it coming. I could feel the tears welling up, but I had yet to let one escape.

I immediately flashed back to the scene in the classroom the day I broke down in front of my students. I concluded that I wanted nothing to do with public crying ever again. There wasn't a chance in hell I was going to do a repeat performance. I refused to be a failure on this issue twice.

So I quickly looked away from the woman who started it all and walked briskly across the stage to the left side of the auditorium. I looked out in the audience and located a few wonderful noncrying people. I stopped and just started speaking directly to these calm, attentive, noncrying audience members. I fed off their calmness and gained control of the emotions that had begun on the other side of the stage. I continued the story. I did not cry.

While I was talking to these awesome noncriers, an idea hit me. I don't know why. I don't know where it came from, and I don't care. I realized that back in that classroom that day, I had not been a failure. It's true that what happened that day was tough. It was raw, elevated, and difficult. It was also, however, not negative. I was not a failure.

What happened in class mostly involved a difficult bunch of positive emotions. I was expressing love for my mother. I was feeling an odd form of joy and elation and determination to help her fight. It was not simply sadness. It was much more. It was best defined as positive, not negative. That class was terribly challenging, but it was not a failure. I built more long lasting bonds with the students in that class than in any other I had ever taught.

When that new understanding hit me, I felt cleansed. I also felt emboldened and renewed. When you're no longer focused on being a failure, you can focus on the principled risk taking that defines personal growth.

I looked back across the stage and made my decision. I was going back to the woman in the blue suit. I strolled her way and locked eyes with her. She was still crying, and she was thrilled to have me back, talking directly to her. I continued talking about my dad as if it were just her and me in the room. It's easy for me to feel emotional when thinking about my dad. He was my best friend, and he was taken too early.

I could feel it start to happen. The pressure welled up in my head, and this time, I chose not to resist the urge. I started to cry—just a little. I finished the story and looked around the massive auditorium. What do you think I saw? I saw hundreds of folks crying, no doubt thinking about someone they loved.

When the gig was over, I had the longest line of people I'd ever seen. They wanted to say thanks, and they wanted to share their stories, just like the one I shared about my dad. It's important to note that the strong response I received that day had little to do with the actual content I was sharing. There are thousands of speakers and writers just like me, addressing the very same issues.

The only difference is delivery. To be clear, I am not encouraging you to start crying publicly. In fact, that might be a huge mistake in many contexts. I am, however, suggesting that you revaluate how you view emotions. The crowd that day could sense authenticity and vulnerability. They appreciated the honest emotion the most. I personally learned a lot about what it means to show your ink that day.

People are starved for real talk, uncensored dialogue, and real emotional engagement. Instead, we go about our lives putting forth an image of ourselves we think is acceptable and appropriate. When we interact with others, we censor because we're socially smart, but we take it too far. We have made progress sensing, reducing, and managing negative emotions. We have also clung too tightly to a view of what it means to be "professional" that dampens positive emotions almost as much as negative emotions.

If you want to feel open and honest, if you want to allow the team to truly understand you, if you want to be more human and authentic, instead of just being a person holding a particular title, you need to embrace positive emotions as much as you work to manage negative emotions.

There are many flavors of positive emotions: joy, gratitude, admiration, interest, sympathy, hope, awe, pride, amusement, curiosity, elation or euphoria...love. These many flavors can each be expressed in multiple ways.

My point is that emotional intelligence will only move from useful to indispensible when we learn to embrace and share the positives just as effectively as we manage the negatives. You don't have to cry, but you can surely share a little joy, interest, and amusement. That's a big part of learning how to show your ink. The team will thank you.

# Story 7

# Moving beyond Simple Stereotypes: *Tattoos Are Sexy*

The pace of life is sometimes a challenge. It tricks us into using too many oversimplified ways of thinking. There are many cognitive shortcuts we use that save us time. The problem, of course, is effectiveness. Saving time does not matter when our thoughts are incorrect. When I think about common thinking mistakes that hurt us at work, one does jump to the top of the list: stereotypes.

A stereotype is an automatic way of thinking about a group that shares some unifying characteristic. This automatic conclusion is wrong more than it's right, and that is why it is so dangerous. Stereotypes are everywhere: cheerleaders are dumb, professors are boring, wealthy people are snobs, poor people are stupid, accountants are not creative, Asian people love math, women are overly emotional, and so on.

Stereotypes are not only common, they're strong. Breaking the cycle of relying on this type of flawed thinking often requires a brave person to provide others with a little cognitive jolt—someone who calls out this type of flawed thinking when he or she sees it. What I enjoy even more is coming in contact with someone who plays against stereotypes: the black kid who loves punk rock, the gay guy who is a huge Republican, the football player who is also a mathlete. These awesome people just make me smile because I know their mere presence on the planet will force a lot of people to question their thinking.

We've all been stereotyped. I know I have. For example, I'm often on airplanes. It's not uncommon—even today when one in five American adults has at least one tattoo—for someone to sit next to me, see the ink, and draw some conclusion about me. People assume I'm either in the military (I keep a bald or nearly bald head), that I'm some type of artistic hipster, or sometimes that I'm a washed-up, middle-aged musician. The most common is the military assumption.

The person sitting next to me spots the ink and says, "So, where did you serve?"

I reply, "Well, I was a bartender at Applebee's in college." When I tell him or her I'm a professor, or now, a professional speaker, the look on his or her face is priceless.

Several other examples stand out in my personal experience. The first involves an incident that happened while I was living in Atlanta, working for Ernst & Young. Several colleagues and I made plans to meet for happy hour one afternoon. I slipped out a touch earlier than my colleagues, walked six blocks home to my place in midtown, and put on a T-shirt and a pair of jeans to loosen up. I then headed down the street to the designated local watering hole. I was the first to arrive.

I took a seat at the bar, and the bartender asked me what I'd like. He seemed like a friendly fellow. I ordered a draft. When he delivered it, he said, "So, what are you up to tonight?"

"Just waiting on a few friends," I replied.

He nodded and walked away to help another customer. No sooner had I finished my first sip of beer that he returned.

This man, whom I'd never met before, leaned over the bar and said, in a somewhat hushed tone, "I think your friends are here."

*How could he know who my friends are?* He nodded to a group of people assembling at a table in the corner. I turned and looked. Skinheads. I was wearing black Doc Martens, jeans, and a T-shirt. I have visible tattoos and a shaved head. I politely explained that I was waiting on few fine fellows from Ernst & Young.

He said, "Who?" Then he realized his mistake and flashed that horrified look that people get when they mistakenly ask a nonpregnant woman when the baby is due. Classic.

Another example actually happened to me several times when I was in my twenties. I'm proud to say that I've had many colorful friends in life. Colorful people make colorful choices. Thus, sometimes, I might be with friends, watching the big game. Other times, I might be with other friends, enjoying a drag show at some dance club. Those were hilarious times.

It was inevitable: 1. At that time, I was still quite the dancer, 2. I wore earrings (still do), and 3. I was in a club around lots of gay people! Sure enough, some terribly nice gay man offered me a beer. I had my routine down.

"Thank-you! Very kind. I'm Todd," I'd say.

He would introduce himself. We'd chit-chat for a minute. I'd down the brew. He'd buy me another. It was only on the second round that I'd somehow let him know I was into the ladies. If I was with a woman, she knew not to interfere. Hey, we were young. Free beer is free beer. I thought it was cute at the time. In retrospect, I know it was horrible. If any of you fellas are reading this, give me a shout. I owe you a beer.

I used these personal experiences to shape how I approached talking about the issue of stereotypes as a professor. That brings me to something that happened one night in class that I'll never forget.

It was the first night of class in a new academic quarter. I was in my second year of teaching MBA students. At this stage of my career, I was still adhering to many social norms. I shaved regularly. I wore a nice jacket to class. I tried to act like an adult and properly meet my students' expectations of what a professor was supposed to be. I had also, thankfully, begun pushing the envelope as an educator. I had slowly begun being more personal, more causal, and more focused on hitting people emotionally, not just logically.

I walked in, wearing my nice sports coat, introduced myself, and quickly ran through my bio and then the course syllabus. Then, the fun began. I jumped into a discussion of what CEOs want when they hire business students. We also talked about what it takes to get promoted. On both lists was the topic of decision making.

Decision making: so common a chore every single day of our lives, yet a topic so overlooked. It is generally just engaged, instead of thoughtfully considered and then engaged. I mentioned several cognitive traps we face as decision makers, and finally I got around to naming my favorite: stereotypes.

I started to describe what they were, why we used them, and the harm they could cause. Then, I stopped and said, "You know what? I want to do a very quick activity that will show you how pervasive stereotypes can be. Here's how this works. I will say a word out loud. I want you to respond to that word with the first stereotypical idea that pops into your head. Don't hesitate or censor—just blurt out your first stereotypical thought. For example, if I said *professor,* you might say..."

I pointed at them, looking for a response, which immediately came in the form of "stuffy," "boring," and "smart." The students started to giggle.

"Good! You're right. Too many of us are stuffy," I added. "OK, you get it—let's go. Ready?"

I say, *"Executive."*

The response was immediate: "conservative," "smart," and "rich."

I say, "Good. How about *jock?*"

"Stupid," "lucky," "entitled."

"What about *cheerleader?*" I continued.

Three people shout, "Dumb!"

"What? All of them can't be dumb!" I joked. More laughs. Then, it was time to turn in a different direction—time to go for the kill.

"OK, how about *prison?*"

"Violence," "bad people," "criminals," "gangs," "tattoos."

And there it was. Sometimes, I had to add one more word, *felon,* before they said it, but they always said it. I stood there in my nice sports coat. I was a young professor. The students did not know me. I had no presence at that time on campus or anywhere else.

"That's a great one," I said in response to the person who said "tattoo." "*Tattoo*—what's the stereotype?"

What followed was awesome. They spouted stereotypes: "redneck," "trendy," "drunken mistake," "criminal," and "will regret." All of these negative labels were being hurled my way. Clearly, the group had loosened up. During this barrage of negative labels in response to the word *tattoo,* a woman in the front row wearing a red sweater cleared her throat and confidently said, "Sexy."

People laughed.

I was standing right in front of her. I took off my jacket, rolled up my sleeves, and showed a few of my tattoos. The class erupted in a fit of laughter at the brave woman in the front row.

The punchline to this story is not that thirty MBA students and I had so much fun watching this poor woman turn six shades of red. Her face did match her sweater, but that was not the point of the activity. I apologized to her.

The point, I explained, was simply to show the power of stereotypes. "I have now done that bit in front of thousands of people. When I say the word *tattoo,* I have heard many negative labels. I have never heard anyone shout 'father' or 'professor' or 'scholar' or any other description that would more accurately apply to me. Why not?"

They got the point. Stereotypes are pervasive. They are powerful. Their accuracy and utility are highly questionable. They represent a filter between you and another person—a filter you can remove, and only then do you see the unique individual standing next to you. You build relationships with unique individuals, not simple labels.

The good news is that with a little thoughtful reflection, you can begin to shake your brain free from reliance on this particular cognitive trap. That's when you realize that tattoos aren't good or bad. It's about what's under the ink.

# Story 8

# Realizing How Others View You:
# *No, Jerry, It's Not Me!*

L ife is strange sometimes. The gap between what we know and what we think we know is often huge. That's part of being human. The only question is about the size of the gap.

This became clear to me while attending the University of Memphis. Well, we called it Memphis State. I grew up rooting for the Memphis State Tigers. While I was a student, they changed the name. Thus, my diploma reads the University of Memphis. Go Tigers!

Like most college students, I had some horrible professors, some acceptable professors, and a small number of truly great professors. My favorite professor during undergrad was a woman I'll refer to as Madeline Davis. Dr. Davis was a treat. She was very much the expert you'd expect as a college professor, but Maddy (as she later told me I was allowed to address her, but not while in the classroom) was much more.

Maddy exuded positivity and passion. She loved being a marketing professor. She knew her content was interesting and relevant, and her animated delivery made her students believe that it mattered. In addition, even though she was very bright, she stopped short of arrogance and clearly had a love of continuous learning. She was delighted when students approached her with questions she'd never been asked. She loved when students would bring her interesting articles they had read in order to get her opinion.

This professor actually cared. She wanted us to learn. She wanted us to feel engaged and feel that our time together had purpose. She would stay after class to entertain more detailed conversations. She would volunteer to help us with our resumes and job searches. She wanted us to leave her class better people than we had been at the beginning.

I was in a relatively small honors program at Memphis, We all needed a certain number of hours in honors courses in order to graduate with honors. The solution at the time was for the dean of the college of business to ask a few professors teaching nonhonors courses to take on a few honors students in their class. The honors kids would be required to complete the normal coursework and an additional honors project of some sort.

Maddy was one of the professors kind enough to work with honors students. The nature of the honors project was up to the student and the professor. This meant that I had to spend more time with Maddy than the other students. I so enjoyed the intellectual stimulation my conversations with her produced. She made an amazing contribution to my development.

It was also a fact that she was a lesbian—at least, I thought it was. Well, we all did. Maddy lived in blue jeans and never wore makeup. She had short, no-nonsense hair. I am keenly aware of the dangers of stereotyping, but nonetheless, I had just assumed she was a lesbian. As we became more comfortable with each other, she did share more about her life with me, but the topic of sexuality was never discussed...

Until it could no longer be avoided. I was out one evening with my girlfriend at an alternative dance club in Memphis called Amnesia. This particular club was one of my favorite places: great music, fun people, huge dance floor. I would describe it as a half-and-half venue—half people part of the gay scene and half a mix of hipsters and college kids.

At one point, I was alone and heading toward the bar for a beer. Then it happened. I spotted Maddy. She was talking to a friend. I didn't know what to do: stay at the bar and risk being seen, thus making her uncomfortable, or leave and have no beer. I stood my ground. I quickly concluded it was no big deal and should not be treated as such.

Sure enough, a moment later, Maddy locked eyes with me. Her face flashed fear for just an instant. Then, like me, she assumed it was no big deal. She smiled and walked over.

"Hey, there—great to see you," she said. "Didn't know you liked this place."

"Oh, yeah, my girlfriend and I meet friends here all the time. Dance a little, catch a show..." I blathered. I'm not sure why I felt the need to tell her I was with my girlfriend, thus clarifying that I was not gay. It's funny looking back on it, but I suppose we're all a little less polished in our youth.

Our conversation lasted only a couple minutes, and it was comfortable. I honestly think the small amount of nerves we experienced had to do with being student and professor. During our chat, she matter-of-factly told me she was gay, but explained that she felt it appropriate to keep that to herself in most situations. I told her I understood and signaled that she had nothing to worry about with me. She gave me a big hug, and that was that. She owned the moment and was proactive and very honest. That's showing your ink.

This was the very early 1990s, and the popular understanding of homosexuality was in transition.

There was of course evidence that people were opening up their minds to see the obvious—that gay people were no different than anyone else. Acceptance in families, churches, and businesses was slowly becoming apparent. However, the operative word was *slowly*. Thus, many gay people chose to stay in the closet or at least segment their lives in such a way that the issue had nothing to do with their professional lives. This was Maddy's chosen path.

Life was good back in the classroom. Maddy and I continued working together as we always had, only now it seemed a little more fun. It's scary sharing a secret with someone, but when you choose well, it's only scary for a few moments. Then it becomes a feeling of comfort, shared understanding, and increased ease. I won't lie. I was the teacher's pet, and I enjoyed it.

I was not, however, the only pet. One of my best friends took several courses with me in the honors program. His name was Jerry. Jerry and I were incorrigible: always sitting in the front, always leading the class discussions. Come test time, we usually had the highest scores. For class projects, we worked together since we were the only honors students. When Maddy asked if anyone wanted to present first, we volunteered. Then, of course, we would stay after to chat with our favorite professor. Needless to say, we were a touch obnoxious, and the other students hated us. We thought that was just fine.

One day after class, Jerry and I were chatting. He said, "So you seemed extra chummy with Dr. Davis today." He called her Maddy as well, but he chose to use her professional name to add a funny, dramatic effect.

"We're both chummy with Maddy. What do you mean?" I asked.

"It looks like you two are a couple in class. You know, like you're dating. Admit it. You're having an affair."

"Dude!" I blurted out. "Are you kidding me? She's our professor—and come on, I mean, she's not really my type. Know what I mean?" Jerry and I had speculated in the past about who she might be attracted to more, men or women. We weren't sure, but we guessed it wasn't the fellas.

Jerry seemed to be kidding, but he wouldn't stop jabbing me. "Just saying, she's a good-looking woman. You two are buds. You're adults. Hey, college is for exploring, right?"

"You're ridiculous. Thanks for clarifying that," I responded to end the conversation.

Later that day while reflecting on my conversation with Jerry, I wondered if I should have just told him the secret. Maddy wouldn't care. Jerry was open-minded, and that subject was a nonissue for him. I could have gotten away with it, and he would have stopped jabbing me. But I knew it wasn't right. I'm not perfect, but when it comes to the issues that really matter, I do try to have integrity. I didn't want to violate her trust, no matter how much Jerry joked.

Soon after, I scored a great internship at a very interesting company called Jimmy Dean Foods (yes, the singer and sausage slinger). I loved my time working there for several brand managers. Apparently, I was doing decent work to support them because when they received funding for another intern, they asked me for ideas. I suggested Jerry.

I knew he would want the job, and I knew the managers would like him. So I told him about the opportunity and suggested he submit his resume. After a few great interviews and one small scare associated with passing his drug test, Jerry was hired!

It was a dream job in many ways. For a college internship, the pay was solid. I got to work with one of my best friends. We were gaining valuable experience (they were not simply having us make copies). The managers all enjoyed us and treated us like colleagues. Yet we didn't have any real pressure since we were not making big decisions. It was a fun and engaging learning environment.

Jerry and I often went to lunch together. Predictably, we'd talk about family, sports, school, and careers. Maddy came up once in a while, but Jerry never again asked any uncomfortable questions—until that fateful day when we decided to have a beer over lunch.

College kids are morons. There we were, enjoying a great internship, learning a ton, and staying out of trouble. Then one day, we decided to do something different. It was a beautiful, sunny day. While grabbing a sandwich at a local deli, Jerry quietly suggested, "Let's get these to go, then go grab a beer at the store and just eat in the car."

For a moment, I resisted. Brow furrowed, I thought, *No! We're working. Who drinks beer during the day?* Then I said, "OK, but just one."

Jerry bought a six-pack. One each turned into three each. The conversation quickly became erratic and hilarious. At one point, he brought up Maddy, and I think he saw me flinch.

I still wanted to tell him what I had learned. I also still wanted to be the kind of friend who keeps his mouth shut. I was convinced that telling him would have no consequences at all. I was convinced he kinda, sorta still thought I had a fling with Maddy. I was also convinced that I should never again drink beer at lunch.

"Dude, look. There's something I need to tell you," I said.

Jerry looked startled. "OK," he said.

"This is a big one, so it really has to be confidential. Seriously. It must stay between us. You cool with that?" I asked.

Jerry half smiled. "Man, I think I already know," he said and took a drink of his beer.

"You do?" I said. I then started to feel more relaxed. He already knew exactly what I was going to say. Of course he did. He either knew she was gay, as most already assumed, or he thought I was going to tell him I had an affair with her.

"What is it you think you know?" I asked.

Jerry said, "You're gay, man. So what. It's no big deal to me."

My jaw dropped, and I choked on a sip of beer. I managed to say, "You think I'm gay?"

A look of surprise washed over his face. "You're not?" he said.

"No! Maddy's gay, stupid!" I yelled.

Jerry erupted in laughter. "I knew that," he said.

"You didn't know! You assumed that. She let me in on the secret, that's all," I replied.

He shook his head. It seemed to make sense to him, though there was still the issue of why he thought I was gay. So I asked.

"I don't know," he said. "You're open-minded about things, and you've got a few gay friends. I just thought it might be a possibility. When I was making fun of you two hooking up, I was just kidding. I figured you both bonded over being gay or something."

We both laughed out loud.

"I guess I shouldn't care that you thought that. It's kinda funny, actually," I said.

"Hell, yeah, it is," he said, still laughing. He raised his beer toward me. "To Maddy."

"To Maddy," I said in return. We finished our sandwiches and beers. Then, for the first and last time in my life, I went to work intoxicated.

It's been over twenty years since that little episode took place. Jerry and I are still good friends, and each time we see each other, reliving that story gets funnier and funnier. Jerry never told Maddy he knew, and she eventually told him anyway while we were all out one evening to celebrate our completion of the honors program.

The whole thing was an amazing gut check for me and a terribly valuable lesson for anyone. You don't know how others view you. There is a gap between what you think they think and what they really think. Sometimes, you might be quite surprised how big that gap is. I know I was.

I don't recommend beer during work hours as a catalyst for next-level conversations. I do, however, encourage you to summon the courage to create a higher level of dialogue with those to whom you're closest. Be open. Be positive. Don't judge. Start talking, but realize it isn't about being paranoid. It's about being as transparent and real as possible. It's about knowing whether or not people see the authentic you.

# Story 9

# Embracing Tough Feedback:

## *Stop Giving Them the Finger*

G rowth is about attitude. It's about effort. It's about focus and determination. It's also about new data. You need to know how others feel about your performance. This is the same at work as it is in any major relationship in life.

That's why feedback seeking is so vital. At work, most people reluctantly accept feedback when they are forced to during the yearly employee evaluation. In life, it's even worse. People are happy to go through their days blissfully ignorant of how others feel about their performance.

That's sad. People who want to be the best version of themselves have to proactively open up to feedback, actively seek it, and thoughtfully consider how to use it. I don't care what your role is—you can be an accounts payable clerk, a father, a barista, a CEO, or a wife. It applies to all of us.

One of the hallmarks of truly successful people is a passion for continuous learning. It's a hedge against assuming you know too much. It is common to see people in midcareer stop seeking feedback like they used to in the first third of their careers, and thus they plateau and stall out. Feedback matters a lot, but it's also true that sometimes feedback hurts. Fine. That's just means you've run into data you can use.

For example, I have a corporate mascot. His name is Danny the Devil Duck. I found the duck some years ago in the bathtub with my two little boys. Danny (named after the iconic character from *Grease,* Danny Zuko) is a tiny red bathtub duck with black devil horns. It's 1 percent evil, 99 percent cool. I used the duck successfully for a few years as a prop for discussing the role of the devil's advocate with client teams. This led me to bring Danny into the classroom. Students loved him.

His popularity grew. At first, he was a symbol for the devil's advocate. Then, he expanded to represent creativity, innovation, and change. Now, he's morphed into simply being a funny symbol of progressive leadership and living. He's my pal. He's snarky. He's cute. I've joked many times that I really hope to be as popular as Danny when I grow up.

Eventually, I had the idea to use Danny as a promotional piece—not just something to hand out at speaking gigs, but something that might be part of a mail campaign. So I started sending out ducks to a few lists

I assembled of folks with whom I'd like to chat. A few gigs quickly materialized, and I was thrilled. I thought, *Yes! Me and the duck are going places.*

Then one day, I went to my office, fired up my computer, and checked my e-mail. Sitting right there in my inbox was a note from a woman whose name I recognized. She was the worldwide head of HR for a massive global firm that you've no doubt heard of. I realized how I knew her name. She was one of people who received my mailing. I smiled like an idiot and began to read.

The first paragraph made my smile grow even bigger. It was short and sweet. The note read, *Dr. Dewett, I am in receipt of the package you sent. I would like to congratulate you for sending something distinctive. I receive a lot of mail, and most things of a promotional nature go straight to the trash, but your mailing caught my eye.*

I began to mentally celebrate after reading the first paragraph. *Here comes a new client!* Clearly, this was going to be the latest confirmation that my campaign was working. Then I read the second paragraph.

It began, and I quote, *As a Christian, I cannot support your choice of corporate mascot. You need to understand that Satan is real, and making light of him with a duck, while no doubt cute to some, is very dangerous.*

After a lengthy multi-paragraph, heartfelt plea intended to help me see the light, she offered some advice. *I think you can still have an exciting mascot that is much more appropriate. Why don't you try a fireman duck?*

I finished reading the e-mail. My initial reaction was disbelief mixed with anger. I felt disbelief because it seemed impossible that someone could take my little rubber ducky so seriously. I felt anger because someone was lecturing me when I felt I had done nothing wrong at all.

So what would you do in this situation? I've asked many folks that question since this happened. The very first thing I did was print out the e-mail. It's now a keepsake. The second thing I did was recognize that making decisions while feeling emotional isn't smart. I turned to another pile of work I needed to address and decided to revisit the note later.

A few hours later, it started bugging me a little. I wanted to respond. *What do I say? Should I even respond?*

A small minority has suggested I should not respond. Another very small minority has suggested I hit Reply and give her a piece of my mind. Most people get it right, though. The answer is to reply and offer a very sincere thank-you.

This woman is a very successful businessperson. Successful businesspeople, especially corporate executives, are extremely busy people. Every minute of every day is claimed by some person or task. I had a keen appreciation for the choice she made to carve out a few minutes of her day to send me a message.

I did not agree with her view of religion. I did not agree with her assessment of Danny. I don't inherently enjoy people telling me I'm wrong. So what. The correct, useful, polite thing to do was to say thank-you.

I replied and briefly explained that she and I might not see this issue identically, but that I genuinely appreciated the time she took to offer me feedback. I told her I value understanding how others view me and my professional actions. I wished her well while resisting the urge to say something clever. I did, however, invite her to call me if I might ever be of assistance. I have not heard from her.

Let's be clear. I don't want to make you paranoid or neurotic, but I do want you to be honest about who you are as a performer at work and in life. Sometimes, you'll like what you find out. Other times, it hurts a bit. I also want you to know that I practice what I preach, even when I sometimes receive feedback I would rather not receive.

For example, several years ago, I was on a stage in Las Vegas, telling stories. At some point, I noted something interesting. I saw a man in the audience I recognized. I knew he was not a member of the company I was speaking to that day. I'll call him Mark. He was a fairly well-known professional speaker who I assumed knew someone at the company. In any case, I knew his work and really respected him, as he was several steps ahead of me in the business. I also knew that, like me, Mark was not a casual observer of communication. Like me, he was able to slice and dice all the variables while watching someone speak. I knew that if I was going to be consistent with what I preached and wrote, I was going to have to approach Mark after the gig and ask him for his feedback.

So that's what I did. I finished the gig, shook some hands, and then raced across the massive auditorium to catch Mark before he left. I admired him, so I was a little nervous. I introduced myself, told him how much I enjoyed his work, and then asked him for his frank take on my performance.

Mark smiled and then backed up a small step. You see, when you are speaking with a stranger or when you are operating in a low performance culture at work, the exchange of frank performance-related feedback often feels like conflict, so people like to create physical distance—usually without knowing it.

He looked at me and said, "OK, sure, I'm happy to do that." He then started by naming a few of my stories he really liked and offered an idea or two about how I might use them even more effectively.

It was pretty good feedback, but I knew what he was doing. People always start with (and often stick to) only the positive feedback they'd like to provide. He was giving me the easy stuff. I thanked him and then gave him explicit permission to give me critical feedback too.

"If there is one thing I can do to be better up there, what might that be?" I asked.

Mark took one more little step backward, breathed in and out, and said, "OK, Todd. Well, you're a big, loud, animated guy."

I thought, *Yes, I'm a big, loud, animated guy.*

He said, "Well, you run around stage the whole time, and you're wearing those glasses."

I nodded and thought, *Did he just state his observation that I wear glasses?* This wasn't the best feedback I'd ever received.

He continued, "You're running around all the time, and you find the need every few minutes to adjust your glasses. So you do—same way, every time, with your index finger." He demonstrated the behavior. Then, he took one final step backward. He said calmly and politely, "You do it that way each time, except when you're holding that remote control clicker in your hands for your presentation slides. When you're holding that clicker, Todd, I'm sorry to say it's not your index finger you use." He paused and then hit me with a zinger. "Today, you gave your audience the bird about fifty times." He showed me exactly what I was doing.

I felt my face flush. I was seriously embarrassed. I lost the ability to talk for a few seconds, but then looked at him and said, "Fifty?" He nodded. I knew what I had to ask next. "Did they notice?"

Mark replied, "I have good news and bad news for you. The bad news is that at least half the audience noticed you were doing this. The good news is that you're a really good speaker, so nobody seemed to care."

Then he told me something I already knew but still really needed to hear.

"It's amazing how much they will forgive of you when they like your message and your delivery," he said. "They see a mistake and forget it almost instantaneously because they are engaged with the performance."

*Wow,* I thought. I giggled a little nervously and thanked him.

He could tell I was a bit surprised. "Don't worry. I see good things for you. You're strong on stage," he said.

"Thanks. That means a lot coming from you," I responded.

"You do, however, need to stop flipping off your audience," he said as he shook my hand and walked away.

It was great feedback from a great speaker. Now, I have to ask you a question. If a highly trained educator and professional speaker is doing something so unacceptable and so unproductive as a communicator that he is completely unaware of, well, how much more likely is it that you are doing something unproductive as a communicator every day that you are unaware of?

Believe me, there's something, but you'll never know what it is until you choose to join the small group of people who occasionally seek honest feedback from relevant people. Start with just one honest confidant who knows you professionally. Ask that person privately for one thing you can do to be a better professional. Then, shut up and listen.

If you want to take it a step further, get yourself captured on video speaking or presenting in a professional capacity. If you've never done this or it it's been years, it will hurt badly. It will also help tremendously. Only then do you begin to see yourself as others do. You might not find that you've been giving your audience the finger, but you never know.

# Story 10

# Creating a New Version of Yourself: *Who Is That Guy?*

M eet Charlie. Businessman. Family man. My father. Also a raging alcoholic. When I think of reinvention and growth, my dad is always the first person to pop into my mind. What started as a relationship I wanted nothing to do with ended with two best friends deeply appreciative of each other and of life.

Dad was a drunk since college, according to what I later learned from my mother. He was, however, a high-functioning drunk—one who gets his work done every day and only drinks at night. Growing up as Charlie's son wasn't a joy ride. While my dad never physically abused us, he was a master of neglect and embarrassment. He was a mean and belligerent drunk. I saw my father asked to leave many public places over the years, from the grocery story to my sporting events. The result was not simply distance between the two of us; I hated him. I made it my life's goal to grow up, leave, and become anything but my father.

Mom was his enabler. She was a dedicated drinker as well, though a simple, funny drunk. She was also deathly afraid of crowds. Thus, she never attended any of my sporting events growing up. Basketball was my main sport, and there were two things I knew about every basketball game I played. The first was that Mom would not be there. The second was that my dad would be there, and he would be problematically drunk.

During my senior year in high school, I was of the opinion that a basketball scholarship would be a good thing. My parents had little money. I later turned down two Division III basketball scholarships when I realized I could likely earn an academic ride, but for most of the year, I was mentally focused on basketball being my ticket.

I took the games seriously. I had a few college coaches watching me. That's what made it extra horrifying when Dad would act up. One night, he outdid himself and actually stumbled onto the court during halftime of a game we were losing. He walked up to my coach and started yelling incoherently. The police escorted him out of the gymnasium and amazingly didn't arrest him. Everyone looked at me with pity. Half of them assumed I'd grow up and follow his lead.

It was very clear that his drinking was progressing. For years, it was just booze at night and coffee in the morning. Then, slowly, it shifted. He began adding a little of his cheap sour mash bourbon to his coffee. The odor was unmistakable. He wasn't fooling anyone. A shot in the coffee was all he needed...for a few months. Then, it was half coffee, half bourbon. Eventually, during my last year of high school, he just decided to skip the coffee and get drunk first thing in the morning.

Then one day he went to work and was served a serious wake-up call. Before he sat down, his boss, Bob, called him into his office. He shut the door. "You honestly think we can't smell that crap you're drinking?" he asked. "Or you just don't care? You're just too lost to care. Here's the situation. I'm going to fire you, today. Right now. I've checked with HR and legal. I've got the documentation I need. You've been warned before, but at this point, you might not even remember that happening. The case is strong, and there's absolutely nothing you can do about it."

Dad sat there, stunned. Welcome to rock bottom.

"Or," Bob said, "you'll go to rehab and clean up. Starting tomorrow. I don't have to pay for this, but I've got the budget. I'd really like to see the old Charlie again." He handed Dad the information about the rehab center. "They are expecting you there tomorrow morning. You'll be there for three months."

Dad took the papers from his hand.

"I think you're worth another chance. The real question is whether or not you think you're worth another chance," Bob continued. "Think about your family, Charlie. What's your answer?"

In tense situations, my father normally would yell, scream, and argue. Not that day. He looked at the papers. "I'll do it. Thank-you, Bob," he said.

"Get your stuff, and go home. Report there in the morning. We'll see you when you get out," he said as he stood up and extended a hand to my dad.

They shook hands. Dad walked with his head bowed to his desk, gathered a few things, and left. He drove home and proceeded to get exceedingly drunk. I came home from school and found him nearly passed out. What was odd was the fact that my mother wasn't angry. In fact, she looked surprised—if not happy.

Dad looked at me and then looked away. He was clearly angry. "I need a drink," he said and then stood up, went to the kitchen, grabbed a new bottle, and walked out of the house.

"What happened?" I asked Mom.

"Your dad's going to get help," she said. Her voice was mildly optimistic.

Dad drank the rest of the night until he passed out. When he woke up, he grabbed his bottle and kept going. He reluctantly put it down on the kitchen counter as we walked out the door to drive him to rehab. When Mom and I dropped him off at the outreach center, all three of us were crying, yet not one of us uttered a word the entire trip.

Dad missed most of my final basketball season. Mom and I promised to visit him during visiting hours. I did. She did not. She cut back on the booze a bit but clung tightly to her normal tendencies. You couldn't get her to go out in public unless it was an emergency. I resisted the idea of going to see him for the first month. Why should I care? I dwelled a good bit on all of the crazy things he had done. I remembered all of the times he had embarrassed me. I thought back to all of the times I had resolved to be anything but him when I grew up.

Then, finally, thankfully, it hit me. It was amazingly brave to do what he did. Yes, he was forced into it, but it was still brave. I imagined it was also lonely. My curiosity grew to the point that I decided to go see him.

I called ahead and left a message for him so he would know when to expect me. I walked alone from the car to the front door of the building with nerves blaring. I'm not sure why. I resolved to be supportive no matter how conflicted I felt. He was standing there when I walked in.

"Hey, Son," he said and smiled.

The tone of his voice was different. His stare had changed. His entire focus felt different. He wasn't posturing at all. He was just happy to see me. I crumbled inside, wanting to believe this was real. He reached out to hug me, and I obliged. I could feel the tears welling up, but I somehow held them back.

After a very short tour, it was time for Dad to report to one of his mandatory meetings. I sat next to him in a circle of chairs with about fifteen other men who were going through the program with him. I felt awkward, like a voyeur, as I watched each man introduce himself, state his addiction, and then share his thoughts about the things for which he was grateful.

Finally, it was Dad's turn. "Hi, I'm Charlie, and I'm an alcoholic," he said. "This is my son Todd. He's graduating high school this year, and next year it's off to college. I'm very proud of his achievements, and I'm grateful to have him here today." He got choked up near the end and began to cry.

That moment changed me. I listened to my dad in conversation with others when the meeting was over. I saw a man who was open, congenial, and clearly quite bright. It very much felt like I was getting to know him for the first time. Within minutes, it became clear he and I had a lot to talk about. The conversation that began that day lasted for twelve more years until cancer finally got him.

Dad finished rehab, went back to work, and later retired and moved with my mother to Florida to be near family. The statistics for alcoholics aren't good. Relapse is as common as breathing. Not for Dad. He admitted he had a problem and needed help and gracefully accepted it. He made amends with everyone close to him, apologizing for all of his poor behaviors.

His example inspired those of us around him. Even my mother found new strength. During Dad's time in rehab, senior night rolled around. During halftime of the basketball game, each senior and his parents would walk out to midcourt together to be recognized by the crowd. Mom could barely go to the grocery store without having a panic attack, so I knew she would politely decline to attend. I was wrong. She held my arm and walked out to midcourt with me that night in front of a packed gymnasium. Everyone knew why my dad was absent. It was a nice moment. I was happy to have her with me. She nearly tore my arm off with her nervous grip, but she made it through with style. Thanks, Mom.

People were quite surprised by Dad's transformation after the program. We discovered he was funny and articulate. What he discovered was a profound appreciation for each day above ground. Genuine gratitude. He became an example to everyone—especially me—about what's possible. In my youth, I used my drunk father as amazing motivation to study and grow and become better in order to have a shot at not being like him.

Then, he pulled the most amazing Houdini act ever. Now, I realized that I wanted to be just like my dad. I wanted to be able to feel deep resolve and change my reality just as he did. We remained best friends until the end.

When I think about Dad's story, I think about the need to not give up on someone. The need to believe in possibilities. The need to be forgiving and helpful just as his boss was. The need to cleanse through heartfelt apologies. The need to be expressive and open since you don't know how much time you have. Most of all, I am reminded that I too am capable of significant growth and transformation—just like my dad.

# Story 11

# Innovating Is Learning: *Marty's MacGyver Moment*

I experienced a situation in a consulting engagement once that taught an interesting lesson. At first, I thought it was about life at work, but soon I realized it was really just about life. The lesson was that personal improvement and creative contributions only result following mistakes, failures, and learning. You have to experiment, fall short, learn, and try again. Improvement is a process!

Managers say they want change, improvement, creativity, and innovation. They are full of it. What they really want is mistake-free and pain-free improvement. Outside of work, people do the same thing. They say they want to get in shape or find a new job, and then one little setback stops them in their tracks. They feel embarrassed and angry and quit. The trick is to weather the storm and learn so you're less likely to screw up again. Setbacks are supposed to be the very things that help you avoid future mistakes.

At a consulting engagement several years ago, this principle came to life in a hilarious manner. I was hired as a coach for a manufacturing company in the Midwest. They had about one hundred million in revenue and growing. The industrial widgets they made were a key component in the manufacturing processes of many other manufacturers in several industries. Their widgets were considered best in class, tops in the industry.

My first day with them started in the president's office. He gave me his take on the company, the team, what needed to change, and so on. He wanted his team to speak up, show more initiative, and create needed change. He claimed his employees would give innovation lip service when chatting with him, but the behaviors were not there. He said he asked for new ideas all the time but got nothing.

Eventually, he took me to a large conference room. Inside, his top team of eleven managers waited for us around a large table.

What followed was horribly boring. They told me about their areas of responsibility, how long they had been with the firm, and so on. Boring! The worst part was watching their body language. It quickly became apparent that these men all respected and revered the president. Unfortunately, the behavioral reaction to reverence looks terribly similar to the behavioral reaction to fear.

After about thirty minutes, I suggested to the president that it might be useful if he left me alone with the team for a while. He looked at me funny but agreed and left. When he left, the reaction of the team was comical. The nonverbal change was huge. People exhaled, pushed back from the table, leaned back in their chairs. They had felt compelled in his presence to sit up straight, pay attention, and avoid fidgeting. Now, they could relax. The status bubble is powerful.

The conversation that ensued was quite different. They got past product lines and strategic projects and began talking more about culture and interpersonal relationships. Professionals often clam up in the presence of consultants, but I'm great at getting people to loosen up. It wasn't me they were worried about that day. It was the boss.

Two weeks later, I was sitting in the president's office, talking about his team, when the phone rang. I couldn't hear precisely what was being said—it just sounded like an angry version of Charlie Brown's teacher. The president was smooth. His words revealed that a product they had sold had broken down, paralyzing the customer's entire manufacturing facility. They wanted a fix, and they wanted it yesterday.

Mr. President hung up the phone. He looked at me and said, "Sorry, Doc. Be right back."

I was worried. He looked like he was going to blow a valve.

He walked quickly out of his office and glanced over the tops of the cubes outside, looking for his target. He found him. Marty was young, strong-willed, smart, and full of creative energy. He was a recent mechanical engineering graduate, and this was his very first job post college.

The president spotted Marty and moved in quickly for the kill. He stopped at the entrance to the young engineer's cube. "Marty! I guess I'll take that forty-five hundred dollars out of your next check. Does that sound good?" He then muttered under his breath, "Special orders..." and turned and walked away. No explanation, no nothing. Jaws dropped across the office. Marty was shell-shocked.

This was the same man who told me people just didn't seem to be speaking up. No wonder! To make a mistake was to receive his wrath.

I followed the president back to his office. He shut the door. There was an awkward silence. I asked what happened. He explained that the company produced a particular type of industrial widget. It was quite technical. Marty was a sales engineer. His job was to talk through many advanced technical issues with the client to ensure the correct product was purchased and produced.

He then told me that Marty had created a custom widget—something the company did not do because of cost and risk reasons. Marty wanted to please the client, but the client wanted a widget that could do a few very unique things.

He continued, "Apparently, Marty thought of a way to act like MacGyver and rig up the machine to do what the client asked for. He no doubt found some buddies in manufacturing to help him. Well, what he cooked up worked. For three months. Then it stopped working. No, it didn't just stop working—it stopped my customer's entire manufacturing process!"

There was silence for a moment.

"Let me guess. It's going to cost you about forty-five hundred dollars to fix the situation," I stated.

He nodded. Finally, he looked at me and said, "Now let me guess. You're going to tell me I didn't handle that correctly."

"Let me ask you," I responded, "how bad was his error? I mean, I'm not an expert in your business, so I'm being honest. We both know there are rules and then there are *rules*. He broke a policy, but maybe we should think about why. It's not like he embezzled funds, know what I mean?"

He erupted. "Special orders are against the rules. First, for our specific product line, they aren't cost effective. Second, they represent a liability we don't want to take on. He knows better. All of our engineers know that's off limits."

"How much of a deviation from standard product design did Marty take?" I asked.

"Not much, really. It was clever, but risky, untested in the field, and it failed," he replied.

I intentionally remained silent.

"What? OK. Maybe I shouldn't have yelled at the kid, but he screwed up with a new, potentially big customer," he said.

"Wait, wasn't that a customer Marty landed with this sale?" I asked.

He didn't answer. I again allowed the silence to continue.

He held up his hands. "Fine, I get it. You're saying I should apologize to Marty. I wasn't serious about that money, either. I just wanted him to understand the scope of his screw-up."

It's amazing what you can get people to say without having to tell them to say it.

Then, I had to give the "bumps in the road" speech. Real improvement requires principled risk taking. Innovations almost never simply materialize. Instead, teams have to try things and experiment to see what happens. They mess up. They take small steps. They create half-baked ideas. It's only through persistent learning that minor—and sometimes large—breakthroughs happen. It doesn't matter if you're working with a product, service, product, technology, or business model—it's a process.

I could see him start to loosen up. He sat back in his chair and relaxed. He smiled. "Maybe I should call Marty in here," he said and reached for the phone.

"No," I said respectfully. "I'm not sure how to say this, but the issue today wasn't just about Marty. Everyone in earshot learned a lesson about innovation. They all heard you out there. They will all certainly remember it later too when they're thinking about going above and beyond for some little risk that might pay off."

His brow furrowed. "You want me to go out there and apologize? He messed up, but you want me to say I'm sorry?"

"You both had a misstep today, but you have the biggest status, and modeling the right thing to do could make a difference. I'd go out there so everyone can hear you. Tell him you shouldn't have snapped. Tell him you're not pulling that money out of his check. Tell him why he should have approached the situation differently. Then, talk about how you can learn from this. Ask him how he can innovate next time smarter, cheaper, safer, and faster.

"That it?" he asked sarcastically.

"No," I said. "You should have a picture of you and Marty taken today, and put it in the company newsletter. Use this opportunity to not only make good with Marty and everyone else who was listening, but go further and turn this into a good moment for innovation at this company. In that article, talk openly about his well-intentioned attempt at innovation and what you learned. Use this as a chance to encourage others to try—and try smartly because innovation matters."

He laughed and added, "Why did I hire you?"

Marty—and everyone else—was intrigued to see Mr. President come back out of his office. I was too. The conversation that followed was therapeutic for everyone. Sometimes stepping up to do the right thing and show your ink is tough, but it's worth it.

Innovation is amazing. It's vital. It can also be messy. Encourage smart risks and embrace learning; otherwise, when you say you support innovation, you're just full of hot air. The same thing applies to your individual life too. I don't want to encourage you to flout the rules just for the fun of it. You do, however, need to push things. That entails risk. Bring it. Otherwise, enjoy being mediocre.

# Story 12

# Choosing Respect over Popularity: *The Man in the Orange Jumpsuit*

The desire to be liked derails many people. It happens a lot to adolescents and teenagers. Kids want to be accepted. They want to be popular. It's almost always true that they wish to maintain or improve their social standing. You never see a popular kid roll up to school in the morning, pause, and think deeply about how to become unpopular.

It doesn't happen. The popular kids want to stay popular. The unpopular kids wish they were popular. That leads to many bad decisions for young people.

Here's the truth: it's not just about teenagers; it's about humans. As adults, we have the same tendency we had in high school. We want to be accepted, if not popular. As a result, we often make some question-able decisions.

Managers do this all the time. They're faced with a decision. They think about their options. They realize that they can choose A, B, or C. After serious thought, they know A is the best choice for the group, but they go with option C because they believe it will be the most accepted and liked option among all constituent groups affected. They look at one group of employees and say to themselves, *They won't hate this one.* They look at another group and say, *They would likely choose this option.* And so it goes. They make the choice that maximizes their popularity instead of making the best choice.

This is a recipe for mediocrity in the long term. You have to admit right now that leadership has noth-ing to do with popularity. That's a dangerous myth. Sometimes, the employees will love your decisions, and other times, they won't. Big deal. Popularity is elu-sive. It is deceptive. It comes and goes. It's fickle and fleeting.

Popularity is not the goal. If you want to be popular, leadership is not your game. A real leader knows that the goal is to make the very best decisions possible for you, the team, and the company; execute them with integrity; and then earn long-term the one thing always better than popularity, which is respect.

I learned just how fast good men and women will turn their backs if they don't like the decision you've made. Many years ago, I was working for a very large consulting firm. One of the projects required my boss and I to take weekly trips from Atlanta to Dallas for many months. It was the two of us and several hundred strangers every week on a very large airplane.

The same routine would unfold every single week. My boss would stand in front of me in line and as we boarded the plane. Next, he would drop his bag in his cushy seat in the first-class cabin. One of the perks associated with his status was flying first class. I wanted that perk. I did not have that perk.

Let me now address the people reading this who have not yet had the opportunity to fly in first class. Ladies and gentlemen, it's a different world in first class. They have wider seats in first class. They have lots of legroom in first class. I'm six feet four and can use all the room I can get. They have a dedicated flight attendant, a dedicated restroom, better food, and free booze. This is the land of milk and honey. Life is good in first class.

My boss somehow found it amusing that he could sit in first class but I could not. Every week, it was the same! He'd plop down in first class and then give me the look. I knew what was coming. You know that partition they use on most planes to separate the first-class cabin from the rest of the passengers? Sometimes, it's a full-fledged wall. Other times, it is an arrogant little curtain.

The week in question, it was a big wall. Either way, the point was the same. The airline wanted you to know you were leaving the good life to go hang with the common people in the back.

The quip always arrived just as I was passing him and headed toward the partition. He just loved to make a joke as I walked past him about how I was walking through what he referred to as the poor portal. It was the gateway from the good life to the thrifty life. He thought this was hilarious. I did not.

Most weeks, his shenanigans bugged me, but not this time. This time, I had what I imagined at the time would be the best seat I would ever have: a seat in the bulkhead row. On many planes, the first row behind first class has legroom for days. Even people taller than me can stretch their legs with no problem. It was the best of the cheap seats, but to me it felt like first class. "Poor portal"—whatever! Let him make his jokes. That day, I did not care. Grinning and comfortable, I pulled out a novel and began to read. There were three seats in my row. I had the seat by the window. I anticipated a delightful flight.

Now I must tell you, this all happened before 9/11. Do you remember life before 9/11? In many ways, life was very different. Life on airplanes, in moments, could be *absurdly* different. Here is but one example.

I was reading my book when out of the corner of my eye, I saw the next person walking through the poor portal to join us in the cheap seats. I looked up and quickly saw the gun, the badge, and the insignia on his shirt. He was a US marshal. He was not alone. With his hand held out behind him, he pulled the next person through the poor portal. That guy was wearing an orange jumpsuit and hand and foot restraints. Where do you think they sat?

Nothing prepares you for this. There is no training. Very little rattles me, but that day, I was rattled. To this day, I still don't understand why the marshal did not choose to sit between me and the fella in the orange jumpsuit. I started to sweat. I knew I was nervous when I realized I had just read the same paragraph in my book ten times.

I admit I was terribly nervous, but I am also insatiably curious, so I knew I had to sneak a peek at the man beside me as we sat there, waiting to take off. I slowly turned my head and realized he was staring right at my book! I didn't know what to do. *What's the protocol? Do you ask him before you turn the page?*

Sweat still pouring, I decided to go further. I quickly sat up straight, turned, and looked back at the couple hundred people sitting behind me. I wanted to know if they understood my predicament. Oh, they did. What I saw surprised me and comforted me. I witnessed the single biggest outpouring of positive nonverbal support that any group had ever shown me. There were hundreds of eyeballs staring at me. Nobody said a word, but their faces were screaming, *Hang in there, fella!* It was oddly comforting to know they all had my back.

My boss up in first class saw this very abnormal thing the government had just forced upon the airline and yours truly. He also saw that there was one unclaimed seat right there in first class. Since the rules were so loosey-goosey back in the day, he quickly talked to the flight attendants, who talked to the pilots, and alaka-zam! They had the answer. The lead flight attendant walked through the poor portal, smiled, leaned over the marshal and the felon, and said to me, "Sir, I apologize for the delay, but your seat in first class is ready now."

Inside my head I screamed, *Yes!* Outside, I tried to be as cool as a cucumber. I unbuckled my seatbelt and quickly stood up. Awkwardly, I eased past the restrained character in the jumpsuit, no doubt looking like an idiot as I tried to avoid actual contact. Once in the aisle, I grabbed my bag in the overhead bin and took off toward the land of cushy seats.

Right before I crossed the actual threshold, I stopped. It hit me. I had something to do before I could proceed. I had to say good-bye to my friends and sup-porters in the back of the plane. So for a second time, I turned around and looked.

What I saw shocked me. Moments earlier, they had been my biggest fans in the world. They were my friends and supporters. Twenty seconds later, they turned on me. Now, they flashed me looks of disgust and betrayal. They wanted nothing to do with me. I was a traitor! The transformation was scary and lightning fast.

So what. Popularity comes and goes. It's fleeting and as unpredictable as the weather. Your goal isn't to overthink about how others feel about you. You should care—but only a little, not a lot. Focus instead on making the very best decisions you can for yourself, your team, and your organization. Then, execute with integrity. That will earn you the one thing always better than popularity, which is respect.

# Story 13

# Focusing on the Now and Later:
## *Dad and Honey Dog*

My brother, Jeff, was always the cantankerous type growing up. Like any good teenager, he gave our mom and dad plenty of things to worry about. It's also true that Jeff accidentally gave my father one of the greatest gifts imaginable.

Jeff was in the midst of his biggest love affair ever. Her name was Tracy. My brother was a ripped-jeans-and-T-shirt guy. Anything fancy-looking made him sick. Then came Tracy. They met at church. His world was rocked by this kind and preppy young woman. The next thing you know, Jeff was walking around in button-down shirts—tucked in—and khakis! We were all quite shocked.

Two weeks after meeting and falling in love, Valentine's Day rolled around. What did Ms. Tracy get him? Chocolates and a sweet card? No. She went to the pound and got him a little puppy. It was a male dog. A black mutt. He was so sweet that Tracy named him Honey. Jeff was still living at home and had to beg my parents to keep him. He swore up and down that he would take care of the mutt and it would not be a burden on Mom and Dad at all.

Two weeks later, Jeff and Tracy broke up. I never really found out what happened. Soon after, Jeff moved out, and he didn't take the dog. With Jeff gone and me very busy, Dad felt he had entered the empty nest stage of life. Honey, or as Dad affectionately referred to him, Honey Dog, was the perfect new companion.

Mom and Dad were friends but didn't share many interests. She was not interested in watching sports on television. She did not like to take walks for five miles or more. She definitely did not like to walk through random fields, attempting to identify which wild weeds and greens were edible and which were not (Dad studied agriculture in college). As it turns out, Honey Dog loved all of those activities!

They became nearly inseparable. They walked together twice a day. Honey sat on the floor next to Dad's chair in the den, either sleeping or watching whatever game Dad was watching on the television. When Dad came home from work, the little mutt's world lit up.

As time went on, I noticed something. Dad was always a voracious eater. He'd eat anything, and lots of it. He did not discriminate. To the day he passed away, I don't think I ever learned of a type of food he would not eat. His friendship with Honey Dog was so close that Dad began doing what many well-intentioned dog owners do: he began feeding the mutt people food.

My father was a smart man, which means he would never eat a meal in the kitchen or dining room when there was a perfectly good television in the den. Dad was old school. He wouldn't just hold a plate in his lap. He was classy, so he used a TV tray.

The routine they developed became legendary around the house and with friends and neighbors. Most dogs have to beg for scraps. Not Honey Dog. He only had to count. Dad was very consistent. It was three bites for him and one for the dog. He placed old newspapers on the floor next to his recliner. It did not matter what the man was eating. Pie, stew, pizza, barbecued chicken, or even ice cream. Three for him, one for the dog. Honey would just sit patiently and watch Dad enjoy his three bites. No begging necessary.

I was walking through the den one day and witnessed the dog enjoying some fine macaroni and cheese thanks to my father. I sat down on the footstool next to Dad.

"You love that dog, don't you, Dad?" I asked.

Without looking at me, he barked, "Of course I do." Then he attacked his mac and cheese once more.

"You'd do anything for that dog, right?" I inquired.

He looked at me like I was a twit.

"Dad, you do realize that you can't keep feeding that dog like a king. If you do, there's sure to be a veterinarian in your future who will be none too happy when he finds out you've been feeding Honey burgers and fries and everything else."

"You're crazy," he said. "We must walk at least six or seven miles every day!" He dismissed me and returned to watching ESPN.

When I first met that cute little mutt, he was already a young adult, nearly fully grown. I would describe him as medium size. His strong little legs shot off the ground about eleven inches before they joined his torso and his tight, trim belly. Fast-forward through several years of fine dining with Charlie, and things changed. Now his legs only seemed to shoot up about five inches before his enormous belly began. The change happened so slowly, Dad couldn't see it happening.

He was a different dog. He used to have limitless energy. Now, he seemed slow and tired. His favorite place to take a nap was always the top of the staircase. Not anymore. He happily slept at the bottom. The most telling fact was the decline in his participation in my dad's famous walks.

For the first few years, no matter where Dad was in our house, he only had to yell, "Honey Dog! Let's go for a walk!" That dog would race to my dad, erupting with happiness at the prospect of yet another walk. Now, Dad would call for Honey, and there was no answer. He had to actively search for the dog.

It was sad. My dad's pal Honey was tired and soon sick. His various ailments piled on. The vet was convinced most of it was due to a life of poor nutrition thanks to my well-intentioned father. I saw my father cry twice in his life. The first was when his mother passed away. The second was the day he had to take Honey Dog to the vet to be put down. Dad knew that he was the major cause of Honey's demise. He wanted to go back and change his choices, but he couldn't.

Every behavior or decision has consequences. Those consequences might be positive or negative, and they might happen now or later. Dad learned a very tough show-your-ink lesson thanks to Honey Dog. Even seemingly small, mundane decisions that feel safe in the short run can pile up to cause trouble over the long haul.

Here are three quick questions I use that might help you avoid this conundrum. First, make the decision to never easily and quickly dismiss feedback. Ever! Dad was far too quick to brush off any feedback about how he was feeding Honey Dog. Second, if you're unsure what the right call is, seek counsel (assuming you have time). The more important the decision is, the more useful a second opinion can be. Finally, ask yourself if you can imagine a better solution to your situation. If you can easily say, "I know a better way to do this," then most of the time, you have to choose a higher-quality solution. In my father's case, this advice might have resulted in Honey receiving less human food.

It's not just our pets, either. This idea clearly applies to our employees and our children. We use too many quick-fix Band-Aids and sometimes make downright poor decisions because in the moment, they feel good and seem easy. If we always remembered to choose quality over expediency, I suspect we'd all have fewer regrets.

# Story 14

# Making Rewards Matter: *Paxon and the Gold Medal*

Here's a question I love asking audiences: "Do we reward people at work too little or too much?" A strong majority always speaks up. "Too little!"

I say, "Wrong! We reward too much."

Here's the thing. Starting sometime in the 1960s, we fell in love with the idea of supporting a child's self-confidence. That's obviously a good thing to do. However, we slowly but surely took it to extreme levels.

Today, all kids are told they are superstars. All children receive some form of participation points. An event can't take place without some well-intentioned adult handing out a trophy, plaque, certificate, or ribbon to some kid who didn't earn it.

In education, some schools have begun to ban grades such as Fs or zeroes in an effort to encourage continued achievement instead of punishing a failure to achieve (both matter). In the process of all of this madness, a few generations of kids have failed to grasp the fundamental elements of success: trying, failing, learning, and trying harder.

Protecting kids from failure is a massively damaging trend. The result is twofold: legions of entitled kids who don't understand success and a country losing economic power because it's staffed by far too many trophy kids (among other problems, of course).

What's the solution? Parents, educators, and bosses must all remember this one vital rule: all recognition and rewards must be contingent on performance. People must earn accolades. Participation isn't good enough. Meeting standards isn't impressive. Being average is not to be rewarded as if it's exemplary.

Allow me to pick on my youngest, Parker. Not too long ago, Parky finished his first year of T-ball. To be frank, he wasn't very good. His team was even worse. At the end of the year, who got a trophy? That's right. Everybody received a trophy! That's horribly wrong.

What did they learn? I can hear some of you say, "Nothing!" The truth is even worse. They learned that they breathe; therefore they are awesome. A terrible lesson. We are doing real damage to these kids.

In fact, we've been doing it so long that companies are now dealing with the first big generation of trophy employees. Have you seen them? They think they deserve a raise and a plaque just for showing up on time for six months. No! We must stop institutionalizing low standards and go back to the basics: connecting the use of recognition and rewards with the production of excellence.

My oldest son, Paxon, learned this lesson the hard way. I came home from work one day, stressed out as always. Even if you love what you do, you can still get stressed out thanks to workloads and deadlines. I stood there in the kitchen and saw my son Paxon, then six years old, in the other room. He saw his father and took off running toward me, full steam ahead, and jumped up in my arms. As many of you know, that little kid's hug melts the stress of the day away like nothing else.

When Pax pulled away from me, I noticed something. Suspended around his neck by a red, white, and blue ribbon was a ridiculously large, shiny gold medal. It was nearly as big as his head! As I readjusted my eyes, I stated the obvious. "Pax, that is an awesome medal. Where did you get that?"

He didn't miss a beat. "Swimming."

Then, I remembered that he had just finished his first season swimming with the community team where we lived. I said, "Good for you, kid. What did you do to earn that medal?"

With no shame at all, he said, "Nothing. We all got one."

I paused and then set the boy down. My smile faded. I bent down to his level and said, "That's unfortunate, isn't it, Pax?"

He looked puzzled. I began to wax philosophical like only an overcaffeinated professor possibly could, explaining what it meant to connect the use of recognition and rewards with the production of excellence. I lectured enthusiastically about striving, real goals, real standards—what it meant to earn something! I was in the middle of a sermon the likes of which you can't imagine when my munchkin decided he'd had enough. In the middle of one of my sentences, Pax turned around and walked away, no doubt convinced his daddy was an idiot.

The next year, Pax was in the second grade. His teacher was a woman I will revere for the rest of my life. Her name was Emily Hendrix.

Mrs. Hendrix sat those young boys and girls down the first day of class and said, "It is so great to see all of you! I want to tell you we are going to have a lot of fun this year—a lot of fun!"

The kids reacted with smiles following her energetic mention of fun.

She continued, "But we are also going to work very hard, and I am going to set a few very tough goals for you."

Little smiles began to fade.

"Let me give you an example," Mrs. Hendrix continued. "Every week, we will take a timed math test. I'll be honest. It's a tough test. Your goal is to try and get every problem finished in under three minutes with no errors at all."

The room was no longer filled with smiles.

"In fact, that is such a tough goal that it's often multiple years before one of my students reaches that level of performance. But if you do," she said and paused dramatically, "this will be yours." She held high a red ten-dollar gift card to Target, the popular retail store.

A room full of second graders gasped. I don't know what ten dollars means to you, dear reader, but I do know that to a room full of second graders, ten dollars is as good as a million bucks! It's a pot of gold at the end of the rainbow. Mrs. Hendrix set the card down on the corner of her desk so that it would remain visible to them every day.

And it began. Weeks one, two, three—kids laughed and had fun, they worked hard, they took the test. Some showed improvement, but none reached the ultimate standard: all problems completed in under three minutes with no errors at all. Weeks four, five, six—same thing. Kids laughed and learned. Many showed improvement, but none achieved the ultimate goal. The ten-dollar, red Target card began gathering dust...

Until week seven, when my son, Paxon Dewett, went to school with a clear head and a good attitude. When Mrs. Hendrix eventually said "go" on that weekly math test, Pax knocked it out of the park—all problems completed in under three minutes with no errors at all.

An hour later, Mrs. Hendrix sat at her desk, grading the tests, while the children sat silently, working on another assignment. She finished the stack and smiled, realizing that one child had done it. With a loud, strong voice, she called, "Paxon Dewett."

Pax is my son, so he assumed he was in trouble. "Yes, ma'am?" he nervously replied.

"Come here, please," his teacher responded.

He got up. She stood as well and walked toward him. She walked out among the desks, took my son by the hand, and brought him up in front of the class.

Pax quickly tried to remember if he'd done anything wrong earlier that day.

Mrs. Hendrix just wanted to make an important point to these young, developing human beings. It would only take a few seconds, but she knew it could have a lasting impact.

Mrs. Hendrix smiled and said to my son, "Congratulations, Paxon!"

Slightly confused, he said, "Thank-you."

"You've clearly been studying, haven't you?"

He replied, "Yes, ma'am."

"You scored a perfect one hundred on the test today. This is for you, Paxon," she said.

Then, it happened. She reached for the card on the corner of her desk. A room full of little second graders gasped, their eyes bugging out. She handed the card to my son, and he floated back to his desk, a man among boys. True story—kids lined up to touch the card. Somehow, it had become magical.

That day when I came home from work, I was stressed out and tired. I stood in the kitchen, and as had happened many times before, I looked in the other room for my boy. When he saw me, Pax took off running, jumped into my arms, and gave me a huge hug that once again melted the stress of the day away.

This time when the boy pulled away from me, I noticed that clutched in his little hand was a red ten-dollar Target gift card. I looked at it and thought to myself, *Man, I hope he didn't steal that.* I said, "Pax, where did you get that gift card?"

He grinned and became animated like only a little kid can. He told me the whole story, beginning with fear of the difficult test, a desire to reach the goal of obtaining the card, and the choice he made to really study hard just as Mrs. Hendrix had instructed him to do. He ended his rant by looking me right in the eyes and saying, "Dad, I earned it."

I was all I could do not to cry right then and there.

Pax, then six years old, now eleven, fundamentally understands one of the most important rules for organizational life and life in general. You have to learn to connect the use of recognition and rewards with the production of excellence.

If you're in charge of awards or part of a group giving them, it's time for an audit. Be honest about who is getting what, when, and why. Listen carefully. I'm not saying you can't give people things. I'm simply reminding you that if you wish them to have any significant positive effect, you have to make them earn it.

# Story 15

# Showing a Little Humility:

## *Angelo the Elf*

Here's a tough lesson for many people to learn. It doesn't matter if you are the nicest person in the world; you will intimidate others if you have a higher status. You've seen it many times. The team instantly hushes when the boss enters the room at work. Members of the church congregation quiet down when the pastor approaches. The players shut up when they see the coach.

This is partially driven by respect. Sometimes it's about fear—sad but true. Most of the time, it is about the status bubble, which is somewhere between respect and fear. The status bubble is the invisible barrier that exists between you and someone above or below you in the hierarchy (at work or in any social hierarchy). I don't care if you are smart, accomplished, kind, open, and compassionate; that might mitigate the effect a small bit, but you can't get rid of it.

What is the effect? In the presence of the status bubble, the person with the lower status will hesitate and censor their comments. It's almost as if they assume the person of higher status is too intelligent or judgmental, so sharing honest comments doesn't seem smart. Even if the individual likes and respects the person of higher status, the status bubble will still make him or her feel insecure. The net result of all of this is slower, less candid, less creative, and less productive conversation.

The bubble is a bear, but there is good news. There is a little-known secret to seriously reducing the effect of the status bubble: sincere self-deprecation and humility. This leads me to a story about a person who made an indelible mark on my life.

When I decided I wanted to be a management professor, I applied to a few top schools. To this day, I feel quite lucky to have been accepted to the management doctoral program in the Mays School of Business at Texas A&M University. It was and still is considered one of the best management doctoral programs in the world.

The place was full of terribly bright people, and I experienced bouts of anxiety and insecurity that were completely new for me. I was smart, but at least two-thirds of the students were clearly smarter. Then, there was the faculty. Some were helpful, and some were snotty, but they were all very talented. Based on their accomplishments, a few even seemed otherworldly—none more that Dr. Angelo DeNisi.

Todd Dewett Ph.D.

A psychologist by training and a management professor by trade, Angelo is considered one of the living legends in the business (at least by his former students!). His list of publications is a mile long. He's been an editor at more than one top academic journal. His work has been cited by others a million times. He's been the president of the Academy of Management as well as a fellow of the Academy. He has also graduated many doctoral students over the years.

Needless to say, due to his stature, all of the first-year doctoral students were afraid of him. We would see him in the halls and want to chat with him about our research or one of his papers, but we'd refrain. You see, in the world of academia, the big names were the equivalent of celebrities to the general public. Thus, we were oddly paralyzed. The status bubble is very real.

Thankfully, Christmas finally rolled around after the first semester of the program. Things were tense. Half of my initial cohort was gone. It is common in top tier programs to see some students quit and others asked to leave. It's brutal but understandable. For the holiday celebration, the management department reserved a large room at a local winery and restaurant. There were white linen tablecloths and beautiful holiday decorations. I sat with the other first-year survivors. They didn't tell us to sit together, but being in the program felt like an odd caste system, as if we were supposed to only associate with each other. We chatted quietly with each other until someone finally looked around and asked if Dr. DeNisi was present. I glanced around.

"Wow, I don't see him," I said. It was a few minutes past the start time for the evening, and his absence was conspicuous, given his status as our fearless leader.

Then, we heard the door to the restaurant open thanks to the sound of holiday bells. We turned our heads. What happened next was a little shocking. A man dressed as Santa Claus waltzed through the door, yelling, "Ho! Ho! Ho!"

It was shocking because the man dressed as St. Nick was not Angelo DeNisi. I will simply refer to him as Mike. Mike was an untenured assistant professor—the low man on the totem pole in the ivory tower. Mike was a great guy but possessed low status, which made it seem odd that he was dressed in such a high-status costume.

Behind him, walking quietly and carrying a big bag presumably full of gifts was a man dressed as an elf. It was Angelo DeNisi. He was one of my heroes, a superstar. He was wearing horribly unflattering green and gold leotards, fake pointy ears, curled-up slippers complete with bells, and a floppy elf hat. It was hysterical. It was also surprising. In the halls of the ivory tower, status matters a lot.

Angelo the elf didn't speak. He just smiled and followed Santa. Santa surveyed the room and directed his elf assistant to one particular table: my table. The table filled with the lowest of the low—the first-year doctoral students. Mike then proceeded to wander the room, spreading holiday cheer as Angelo walked to where we were seated.

I wanted to laugh, but I didn't. How could I laugh at this intellectual giant? Then I looked at his goofy, pointed ears and the silly grin on his face. I giggled just a little. He approached the young female student seated next to me, pulled out a small gift from his bag, and handed it to her.

"Merry Christmas," he said. "Thank-you for your contributions to the department. Enjoy the evening."

With his shoe bells ringing, he casually approached every person at the table. His simple act and his sincere kindness and gratitude changed how all of us viewed him. In less than one minute, he had ceased to be the unapproachable intellectual giant and had become human. He laughed at himself and his status by assuming the lowly role of the elf. He then chose to serve a table of people so clearly beneath his standing. He did it with a smile.

After visiting each table, announcements were made, a few awards were handed out, and dinner began. Angelo remained in costume the entire time. By the end of the evening, he no longer seemed out of reach. He seemed goofy, real, and approachable. What an amazing show-your-ink lesson he had taught us.

Just over a week later, the new semester began. Within days, it happened. I was walking down the hall somewhere, looked up, and saw the legend walking toward me. For a split second, I felt jitters as I sensed the weight of Angelo's reputation. Then, I flashed back to the dinner party. I remembered how silly he had looked. I recalled how genuinely kind he had been to all of us. I thought about the clear point he had tried to make that night. We had different titles and different accomplishments, but at some level, we were all in this together as colleagues.

The status bubble popped.

"Hey, Dr. DeNisi," I said.

"Todd. How's it going?" he replied.

I had no idea the man knew my name. "I was hoping to run an idea for a paper by you."

"Let's hear it," he replied.

I dropped any apprehensions and jumped into my first ever conversation with Dr. Angelo DeNisi. We had exchanged pleasantries before but never really talked. By the end of our hallway chat ten minutes later, I felt enlivened. He had given me several issues to consider that might inform the question I was pursuing. He pointed me toward several theories and research streams worth considering. Then, he did something that shocked me.

He said, "You know, it's never too early to start thinking about who you want on your dissertation committee."

This was a compliment of the highest order. He was suggesting he might be open to serving on the committee. A couple years later, when I asked him, he agreed. Angelo was an incredibly valuable resource in his role as chair of my dissertation committee. After successfully defending my dissertation research, he was the individual who instructed the university to confer upon me a doctoral degree.

I often wonder whether or not I'd be Dr. Dewett if it were not for Angelo dressing up like an elf. He showed me that with creativity and sincerity, the status bubble doesn't have to be such a burden. His example heavily influenced how I managed my students in the years to come, how I treat people professionally, and how I train others. Thanks, Angelo!

How will you use this concept? I challenge you to identify one clear situation where the status bubble is causing a problem. Get creative about what you might do or say to help others see you as more human and approachable. You don't have to dress up like an elf, but you do have to take a risk and do something different than what you've been doing.

# Story 16
# Demanding Positive
# Perspectives: *Charlie's Epiphany*

Pushing others to new levels of performance is a challenge. Above all else, it requires a positive perspective. I think we all understand the importance of a positive perspective, but do we really appreciate it? I suspect we do not.

We all face challenges, hurdles, and failures. We can choose to view any situation negatively or positively. You can look at a setback as a failure, something embarrassing. That's the glass half empty perspective. It's a focus on the downside. If you want to, you can look at a setback as an opportunity to learn and take a huge step forward on your next effort. That's the glass half full perspective. It's a choice to focus on the upside.

We all know the smart move is to adopt a glass half full approach. This idea has been so common for so long that people unfortunately take it for granted. It's as if the idea that a positive perspective is useful has become some sort of pop psychology. People acknowledge it if asked, but they don't view it as interesting and important.

That's a shame. Research and common sense suggest that maintaining a positive perspective and sharing a positive perspective with others is just short of magical. It's free too. You're welcome.

For me, this notion has always been important, but I will admit there is a difference between understanding something logically and feeling it emotionally in your bones. That's why I owe my dad. (Well, I owe my dad for a lot of things.)

I had lost both of my folks to cancer by the time I was thirty-eight years old. As tough as that was, I also realized that if you're paying attention, it's amazing how much you can learn during your most difficult times—*if* you're paying attention.

The thing is, when tragedy hits, most people are too lost, wallowing in the negativity, to learn anything meaningful. We all have negative moments. We all feel powerless. We all lose focus for a time. If we're lucky, someone helps us see clearly once again. Here's the story of how my father did that for me.

I was in College Station, Texas, sitting at kitchen table, writing a paper as a part of my doctorate program. The telephone rang. I picked it up. "Hello?"

I heard my mother's voice, but before I could say anything, she was gone.

A man got on the line. He said, "Todd, this is Dr. Wently. I'm sorry, but your mother is choked up and can't speak. She handed the phone to me."

Then, I remembered that my father, Charlie, was scheduled that day for what we thought was routine gallbladder surgery.

Dr. Wently continued, "Son, we went in to look at and hopefully fix your father's gallbladder. Unfortunately, what we discovered was that it was malfunctioning, not in and of itself, but as a result of something else. Your father has cancer in little bits and chunks all over his abdomen, and there's absolutely nothing that can be done about it. I'm sorry."

If you've ever received information of this nature, you know that it hits you like a ton of bricks. It takes the air right out of you. I gathered myself and, believe it or not, thanked him for his forthright manner. I am keenly appreciative of the need for candor. It is one of the defining characteristics of high performing teams, and quality relationships in general.

Then I asked him the obvious question. "Doc, how long does he have?"

"This is serious, so I won't mince words. I'd be surprised if your father lived another three weeks. Son, you need to get on an airplane and come see your dad," he said.

I thanked Dr. Wently and hung up the phone. Dad was seventy-three years old. Wow. I then called colleagues from Texas A&M and asked them to cover courses I was teaching. I hopped a plane to Tampa, where my folks lived.

When I walked in the door of their house, I did what you might expect me to do. I hugged and cried with my mother and father for a few minutes. Then, Dad and I walked out of the house together.

I'm a serious extrovert, and I am my father's son. I can talk all day long. My dad was an Olympic-level extrovert. When the two of us got together, it was a fierce competition for airtime.

My most precious memories in life were during my college years because to save money I stayed at home and lived with my parents. This gave me a ton of time with Dad that I otherwise would not have had. Newly sober, the thing that had kept Dad sane was walking—a lot of walking, every day. He was kind enough to include me when I was around. Dad would walk up to me with a thin, white rope in his hand and ask me if I wanted to go chew the fat. The rope was the makeshift dog leash Dad used. He was excessively cheap. "Chewing the fat" was Dad's way of saying "let's go talk." And we did.

Father and son. Two world-class extroverts talking about all aspects of life: business, religion, politics, careers, sports, the crazy neighbors. I'm not sure we ever solved any problems on those walks, but we had a blast as father and son chewing the fat.

That day in Tampa, we walked out of the house, and for the first time in our lives, neither one of us said anything. We just walked. This was surreal, given our past. An hour later, we were still walking, and neither of us had said a word. My seventy-three-year-old father became tired and decided to sit down on a bench by a pond in his neighborhood. I sat down next to him, and we continued not talking.

I must admit, I was doing what most of us do for a period of time when we are faced with difficult information we'd rather not deal with: I was marinating in the negativity. I was wallowing in the pain, despair, anger, and confusion. While I was stewing in this negative state, something odd happened. I was shaken out of it by a sound that surprised me. It was the sound of laughter.

I looked next to me, and there sat my father, laughing at me. Giggling, really.

I asked the obvious, "What are you laughing at, Pop?"

"You're sitting over there, thinking a bunch of negative stuff, aren't you?" he asked.

I said, "Yes, I am."

"I understand that," he continued. "I've been doing too much of that in the last few days while I waited for you to get here. I was mad, angry. I did that. I'm done. There's a better way."

I said, "Yeah?"

"Yeah. I could be angry. There's plenty to mad about. I could be mad at God, mad at life, mad at everything. You know why? Because I'm not going to watch your kids grow up the way I thought I was. I could be mad because I'm not going to go home many more times and see that woman who I still love after all these years. I could be mad because I'm not going to walk out to this pond many more times and chase fish."

He paused. "I could be mad. I did that. I'm done. There's a better way."

"That right?" I asked. "How so?"

"Well, the doctors seem quite clear. I have this condition, and there is absolutely nothing that can be done about it. But you know what?" he asked.

"What, Dad?"

"How I choose to feel about it and how I choose to think about it is entirely, wholly, completely, and utterly up to me. If I wanted to, I could be mad. I did that. I'm done. There's a better way. Instead, I choose to be happy, not thrilled. You know why?" he asked.

"Why?" I responded.

"Because I'm sitting here doing the thing in life I love most. I'm talking to my best friend. And when we're done, I'm going to go home and eat whatever that woman cooked because it's always delicious. Tomorrow morning," he continued, "I have a good shot at putting two feet on the floor, and when I do, I intend to walk out to this pond and chase some fish." Then, he reached out his hands as if he were grasping something amazingly important and said, "That's my choice."

It was amazing to watch a person in his situation make the choice he made. He taught me that day that reality is very much a choice. They gave Dad three weeks if he was lucky. He lived for the better part of two-and-a-half years—much of it in great spirits, through many rounds of chemotherapy—before the cancer finally got him.

Professionally, I have more flexibility than most, so I was privileged to be with him for much of that ride, including his last moments. What a blessing. During that journey, his doctors pulled me aside many times and told me that though they could not prove it the way they wanted to scientifically, they knew the explanation. They knew in their bones that the best explanation for his unexpected longevity was the fact that he made the choice—every day—to frame his situation as positively as possible.

Now it's your turn to learn from my dad. Go to work for the next week, and at every meeting you attend, take notes. Specifically, note how many times someone chooses to frame their comment positively or negatively. Any comment, issue, idea, or situation can be shaped positively or negatively. As you watch, you might be surprised by how often we unconsciously choose a negative perspective. If you want to be worth your salt as a leader, your job is to reverse that reality so that the average perspective is positive. Research suggests that when you do, over time, your team will make better decisions and will be more productive.

A positive perspective focused on gratitude, opportunity, and possibilities is a choice. Who knows. Making that choice might change your life. Thanks, Dad.

# Story 17

# Encouraging Big Thinking: *Now What's Possible?*

Goal setting has long fascinated me. The most interesting aspect isn't that many people fail to use this basic but terribly useful approach to self-improvement and achievement. What's more amazing is how few have discovered the power of dreaming—not just goal setting, but setting clearly audacious goals. Harder, yes. More risk, sure. Worth it? You bet. It leads to a life of stretching, trying, chasing—and sometimes even reaching—your potential.

Common sense and good scientific research told me that goals work, but that's where common sense and science split up. The studies suggest that goals must be reachable or reasonable. This is to avoid setting goals so high they cease being motivational and begin to actually hurt motivation.

Generally speaking, this makes sense, up to a point. When you think about this logic, doesn't it follow that you're locking yourself into safe and incremental progress? I believe it does. Living a life fully examined requires more. I can promise you this much. If you don't occasionally set an audacious goal, your performance will not be audacious. To maintain balance and sanity, you can't make every goal audacious. How about one in ten? Or maybe one every three or four years?

While I was in graduate school as a young married person, I understood this idea. That's why I was in graduate school. However, there are levels of understanding. Sometimes a certain experience will take something you know or believe and make you understand it at a deeper level.

An experience with my wife at the time did just that for me. Laura was a great person. She was also a red-headed, freckle-faced asthmatic. As a child, she was no stranger to the emergency room. She had regular asthma attacks and always had to carry her inhaler. The condition was bad enough when she was young that playing sports was not an option. It was just too dangerous and uncomfortable.

Thankfully, as an adult, she had grown out of the condition as many lucky people do. By the time we met in our late twenties, she only had the rare mild attack.

She carried her inhaler mostly for safety. However, the condition was present enough that she continued to steer clear of serious physical activity. Laura loved to walk but was extremely cautious about anything more.

Soon after falling for each other, I quit a nice job at Ernst & Young and began a doctoral program at Texas A&M University. Laura and I lived together in a tiny apartment and were married months after arriving in Texas. I loved the program, but it was brutal. I worked very long days, seven days a week, for the first two years. I basically lived at the office.

When I would finally force myself to leave and go home, I'd typically find Laura wrapping up her evening. At the time, she was an elementary school language arts teacher, so wrapping up the evening meant wrapping up grading papers and writing lesson plans. We'd chat for a few, and then, most nights, I'd take off for a run. That's funny now, since I'm a pudgy, middle-aged guy, but at the time, running helped me cope with the stress of the program.

It was a short route I normally followed, just over three miles around campus. I often asked Laura if she wanted to join me. She would decline. That's not accurate. She'd bite my head off.

"You know I have asthma! I can't run!" she'd protest.

I honestly didn't know whether or not it was safe for her to go jogging, but I'd seen her walk and hike with so few asthmatic incidents that I thought it might be worth a try. When she turned me down, I didn't argue. I did, however, continue to ask her if she wanted to come along.

One day, she surprised me. I was walking through the living room one night and asked her to join me. I didn't even stop walking since I knew the answer.

"Absolutely. Let's do it," she said.

I stopped in my tracks and looked at her. "Really?"

She nodded and ran to the bedroom to change. We stretched for a couple minutes and headed out the door. I was nervous and excited. She was more nervous and excited. Off we went—very slowly.

I realized quickly that this was going to be a long three miles. So be it. I was thrilled to see her run. She looked like she might pass out after one mile. I started running backward at one point to talk to her and motivate her. That seemed to annoy her, so I turned around again and simply looked back every couple of minutes to make sure she was still going.

One foot in front of the other, she kept going. She finished mile two, then mile three. She ran the entire course! Very slowly, but she did it and never stopped once. As we walked a bit to cool down, her endorphins kicked in, and she felt more exhilarated than she had in years.

"Woo-hoo!" I recall her yelling a few times. This was a major deal, a huge accomplishment mentally and physically. We laughed and carried on for the remainder of the evening. She vowed to go running with me more often, even if it was slow. She made good on that promise and ran with me many more times. She had come a long way from the emergency breathing treatments at the ER as a child.

Fast-forward several years, and I'd taken a job as an Assistant Professor of Management at Wright State University in Dayton, Ohio. My running days slowly faded as I became lost in my work and busy with home chores—and then parenting chores. Little Paxon arrived. Laura never said a word to me about the fact that we stopped running. She was very happy in her new role as mommy and seemed content taking walks with her other mom friends in the neighborhood.

One night, I was cooking dinner when Laura walked in.

"Honey, I've decided to run a marathon. Just wanted you to know," she said.

I was skeptical. Because I did not want to sleep on the couch, I censored myself and simply said, "What? Wow, that's amazing. Where did this come from?"

She explained that one of her friends had told her that anyone could run a marathon. You didn't have to be an Olympian. You only needed to train correctly. Then, Laura whipped out a book entitled *Marathons for Beginners*. She pledged to follow the plan it provided.

Laura knew what she was doing. She told me, Mr. Motivation, that she was going to run that marathon. There are different ways to commit to a goal. You can think about it—that is good, but thoughts are fleeting. You can write it down in some fashion. That makes it far more like a contract, increasing the odds of goal attainment. Or you can opt for the highest level of commitment—what I call "going public."

You find a person you trust who knows your ability in the area of performance you're targeting. Give them clear permission to monitor you and check in with you to ensure you're making progress. You do this, and your odds of success soar. She told crazy, goal-focused me that she was going to run a marathon. There was no way she was going to fail and continue to look me in the face day after day. Failure was no longer an option.

I do admit to having my doubts at first. This freckle-faced asthmatic had never run more than three miles in her life—slowly. I did, however, wish her well, and I wanted to see her achieve her goal.

What happened next was just astounding. In College Station, Texas, we ran in warm weather. Now we lived in Dayton, Ohio. She began her training in the winter for a spring race. I wanted to be a decent husband, but

I never once thought about offering to train with her. Maybe one-third of the time, she trained on a treadmill at the local YMCA. The rest of the time, she was running at night, in the dark, in the cold.

I was amazed at her resolve. She followed the progressively difficult plan the book suggested week after week. First, it was only a few miles. Then, she was running ten, then eighteen. She ached. She got shin splints. She developed a few huge blisters. She kept going. Holy cow. I started to believe that 26.2 miles was indeed possible.

A few months later, young Paxon and I accompanied her to Cincinnati, where she successfully completed her first marathon, the Flying Pig Marathon. She never stopped. Watching her run that race was truly exhilarating. Paxon cheered from his stroller. I stood behind him and yelled and screamed.

The look on her face when we rendezvoused later was priceless. She looked happy, but more interesting to me, she looked confident. She felt like a badass. Most of our celebration dinner that evening was just her recounting how she felt and what she was thinking over the course of the race. Early in the race she was thinking, *Come on, come on! I can do this.* She described how that slowly changed after she passed the halfway mark to *Wow, I'm going to do this!*

I had long been a goal and achievement junkie. More than once, I had slipped into coaching mode to push her as well, but that day, she was the coach. I was just happy to be along for the ride.

At one point during the meal, she said, "I can't believe I actually did it. I mean, it wasn't long ago I thought three miles was a nice accomplishment."

"I know," I replied. "It's honestly amazing what you can do when you put your mind to it."

"Kinda makes you wonder what else is possible that you thought was impossible, doesn't it?" she said. With that comment, she taught me one of the greatest show-your-ink lessons ever. Goal attainment is awesome, but allowing goal attainment to open up your mind to conceive even bigger dreams is the real key.

She kept dreaming. Since then, she finished her MBA, changed careers, ran another marathon and multiple mini marathons, and now wants to try a triathlon. I believe she will. Laura now believes that if you're going to dream, you might as well dream big because you never know what you're capable of until you try.

We proved that as a couple not long after. Three unexpected and difficult things happened. Her father went into the hospital with pneumonia and died suddenly two weeks later. Laura herself was hit by a car while standing in a grocery store parking lot. She required three surgeries and nearly two years of rehabilitation to return to her old self. Finally, my mother called and informed me of a lump on her throat. She passed away two months later. All three incidents happened in a span of about a year and a half.

Your personality and many of your behavioral tendencies are formed and written in concrete during adolescence. However, certain large or life-changing events can cause shifts. These three events pushed us to adopt new attitudes and to start new conversations about who we were and what it meant to chase happiness in this short life.

Laura and I had been clear opposites when we met and married. I am an extrovert. She is an introvert. I find politics and religion fascinating. She does not care about either. I love to read the news. She never reads the news. I am more expressive. She is more conservative.

Today, we know what many others know—opposites attract but don't usually fit well. We learned this the hard way. Our incompatibility basically resulted in pursuing two different lives while living under the same roof. Neither of us was having any fun.

Then, things changed. Her newfound perspective following the marathon changed her. The combined power of those three difficult and unexpected events changed both of us. We found ourselves in a place where having tough conversations with immense candor was possible while being positive and supportive of the other person at the same time.

When we started what became transformational con-versations, it was Laura who first said, "You know, what we become is completely up to us. How we define ourselves is our choice." She was brave. I realized she was correct.

Until that moment, we had both been focused on tra-ditional concerns: how others would view our divorce, the impact on the children, financial issues, and so on. Following the moment she uttered those words, a dif-ferent conversation began. In short order, we had for-given each other for every unkind thing we'd ever said, done, or even thought. We worked out sensible solu-tions financially with no arguing at all. Most important, we figured out how to ensure that our two boys never experienced our divorce as the negative event most children are forced to endure.

Above all else, we agreed to be positive, stay friends until the end, and choose to live life in pursuit of hap-piness. We imaged that through legitimate positivity, anything was possible. Fast-forward several years, and I'm thrilled to report things have worked out exception-ally well (and yes, she approved this story). We're both involved as happy coparents to the boys. We're both chasing genuine happiness in our own ways. In addi-tion, we're both still close friends who visit and break bread often and will continue to view each other as fam-ily for the remainder of our days.

Don't get me wrong. I don't want to suggest there were not bumps along the way. There were a few, but they were surprisingly minor. I'm grateful for the transformation we underwent, and I give Laura the lion's share of the credit.

I always believed that more is possible, that audacious goals matter—in theory. Then we faced a marriage falling apart. Thanks to the power of forgiveness, a desire to be genuinely helpful, and a relentless focus on positivity, we figured out how to turn theory into practice. We became much better versions of ourselves. Thanks, Red!

Seriously, people. If you don't dream audacious goals, what's the point?

# Story 18
# Teaching Positively: *Way to Go, Coach!*

When I think about managers as teachers and coaches, I'm immediately reminded of the power of emotion. Our words and behaviors are wrapped in emotion. The nature of the emotions used is every bit as powerful as the words and behaviors themselves.

I like to remind managers that emotions move like a virus. They're contagious. They move from person to person and group to group surprisingly fast. There is a troublesome finding that you should be aware of: negative emotions tend to move faster and stick longer than positive emotions. Thus, some groups build up so much negative emotion, they hit a tipping point, and the negative emotions smother the positive emotions, creating a less-than-fun place to work.

I always love asking audiences to indicate by show of hands how many of them have ever worked with a serious jerk. It's amazing: a majority of hands shoot up. The people in the audience who raise their hands go back in their minds to the time they were still working with the jerk. Without any conscious thought, they react to the person. In an instant, they re-experience the negative emotions associated with the person and shoot their hands in the air.

To be clear, by *jerk,* I'm not referring to someone who engages in violence or breaks laws. That would be a criminal. A jerk is someone who is consistently unpleasant to you and others. He or she is excessively selfish, demeaning, insensitive, or offensive.

So then I say, "Wow, that's a lot of hands. What a shame. Jerks are no fun. They're a disease that kills morale and eventually productivity. So, answer this question for me. How do you explain the existence of jerks at work?"

Normally, a few people speak up and state the sad, obvious truth: we allow them to exist. More specifically, leaders allow jerks to exist. Why do they do that? Once in a while, it's because they are unaware of the jerk or ignorant to the corrosive impact a jerk can make. It's also true that sometimes they are simply avoiding conflict.

However, the most common explanation is that they justify bad behavior because the person is good at what they do. I've had this conversation—sometimes it's an argument—with many executives. Maybe two-thirds of the time, they agree with me: no amount of great talent justifies consistent jerk behavior. About one-third of the time, they wax philosophical about the beauty of real talent.

They drastically underappreciate this simple fact: a talented jerk hurts you while helping you. They upset others and reduce the impact of the collective talent of everyone else on the team. Great talent can be blinding. It stops some observers from seeing the damage being done.

Jerks ruin chemistry. The real war isn't for the best talent. It should be a war for the best chemistry. I'm not suggesting that mediocre talent can win the day. However, in sports or anywhere else in life, a good team is capable of beating a "better" team when they have great chemistry and thus execute more effectively.

Sometimes, professionals agree with me, but then they throw out what I've decided to call the Steve Jobs defense. They say, "Steve Jobs was well known as a disagreeable, egomaniacal jerk. So what? Nobody can do what he did, so you just have to accept that sometimes he'll be a jerk." For the record, Steve Jobs is one of my heroes, and yes, he was most definitely a jerk on occasion.

My response is simple. I ask, "How common is it to find a Steve Jobs? This is a man who changed multiple industries." They concede it is exceptionally rare. I continue, "Fine. Let's say—and I'm being generous here—that one percent of jerks are geniuses like Steve Jobs. I agree that we should find a way to tolerate their eccentricities. Now, let's talk about the other ninety-nine percent who really do need to be called out and contained." People typically agree with me when the argument is framed in this manner.

I have a bit I've used for several years now with live audiences. It's designed to demonstrate the fact that negative emotions are so powerful and the negative images they create are so enduring. After talking about jerks and chemistry versus talent, I tell them I want to give them an example of the power of negativity and negative emotions.

"In a moment, I'm going to say a name out loud for all of you to hear. Most of you have heard of this person. It's a him. Some of you will know a lot about him, some not as much, but most of you will know him. Now, when I say his name, I want you to quickly say out loud the first descriptive word that pops into your head. Don't censor. Just be honest and loud. OK?"

The anticipation builds as I slowly give the instructions. People look a bit nervous since they just agreed to react to a person's name with no knowledge of how they will actually feel about the person. That's a little risky, and it does lead to some people not responding, but most do.

Finally, I say, "Coach Bobby Knight."

I've used this activity with thousands of people, and the reaction is the same group after group. When people hear the name of the man often referred to as the General, they aren't confused about how they feel. The top three answers are quite consistent. The third most common reaction is "choke." I'll leave it to the reader to look up the details. Suffice it to say Knight's temper got the best of him on more than one occasion. When one of those incidents showed up on video, it was the beginning of the end for the coach. The second most common response is "chair." Again, for the uninitiated, it won't be hard to find some good video to explain.

The number-one most common response has been terribly consistent. Sometimes they say it quietly if the group is smaller. If there are a few thousand in the audience, the response is more like a roar. They yell, "Asshole!" Then, they giggle nervously.

I say, "You realize that I did not ask you for a negative description, correct?" They get the point. Nobody ever screams, "Winner!" or "Awesome!" No one jumps to their feet to say anything positive. They say what comes to mind. "Asshole!" Negativity sticks hard.

It's important for you to know that I revere Bobby Knight. The only sport I was serious about growing up was basketball. I enjoyed the Hoosiers. I was well aware of Bobby Knight. Fast-forward to today, and I feel sorry for him. He's one of the best basketball coaches in history. He's now enjoying a stint as a color commentator and seems to have calmed down, but the damage is done. "Chair!" "Choke!" "Asshole!"

Knight is third on the list of coaches with the most wins in men's NCAA basketball. He has more NCAA men's basketball appearances than any other coach. He is the only coach in history to win the NCAA, the NIT, an Olympic gold, and a Pan American Games gold. His is one of three men to have played on and coached a winning NCAA championship basketball team (Ohio State and three national titles with Indiana University, respectively).

From my perspective, there is something far more impressive to me than his wins on the court. Knight was well known to run clean basketball programs. Aside from his epic anger fits, he showed lots of integrity. As a result of his belief in standards and hard work, his players graduated with college degrees at a far higher rate than the players of nearly all of his contemporaries.

He is a Hall of Fame coach who has been recognized as one of the greatest ever. Yet, the crowds scream, "Asshole!"

Inevitably, after I wrap up that part of the speech, an angry Bobby Knight fan will speak up. They don't raise their hand. They just speak up. They say, "Lookee here, speaker boy," or something similar. "Kids knew what they were getting into when they went to play for Coach Knight. There's no mystery there. Everyone knows what he's like."

I say, "Really?"

"Yeah!" he or she responds belligerently.

I continue, "OK, give me a quick show of hands. How many people in this auditorium are married?" A majority raise their hands. "Did you really know what you were getting into?"

People erupt in laughter.

"No! You did not know what you were doing. There are some things you don't understand until you do them. You can think about it, talk about it, or read about it, but you won't get it until you do it. Getting married, having a child, losing a loved one, going to war. You don't understand these things until you experience them. I don't care how silly it sounds, but I think playing for Coach Knight might go on that list." That's the first thing I say.

Then I ask, "Have you ever heard of a man named Larry Bird?" Most people immediately recognize the name of the legendary basketball great. "I loved him. Oddest-looking man ever to play basketball, but I still had his poster on my wall for years. You know why? Because that man performed to his potential better than any other athlete ever. Did you know that the man they call Larry Legend once had the chance to play for Bobby Knight at Indiana?

"Many fans of the game are not aware of this fact. Larry was there on scholarship. Apparently, he felt lonely and out of place on such a huge campus, having grown up in a small town. Very early in his time at Indiana, he was walking across campus with friends when he saw Coach Knight approaching. He said hello to his new coach for the very first time. Knight didn't respond. He just walked on by, too self-important to even acknowledge the young man. It had been less than a month since he arrived, but Larry made`his decision. He didn't like his college experience, and he didn't like his coach's personality. So, he quit.

"He went home to French Lick, Indiana. For the next year, he enrolled in a community college and made money by mowing lawns and driving a garbage truck. The next year, he enrolled in a school nobody outside of Indiana had ever heard of and put them on the map with his basketball skills." I like to ask the audience, "Do you know the name of that school?"

With few exceptions, someone knows that answer and says, "Indiana State."

"That's right. Indiana State," I say. "And it's likely the only reason you know that is because Coach Bobby Knight is a serious jerk. Isn't that amazing?"

I tell my audiences the truth. Knight is interesting, smart, a winner, and a true legend. His basketball acumen was second to none. That's not the question. The real question is, can you imagine what that man would have accomplished if his standard operating procedure was positive on average instead of negative on average? If he was as caring as he was demanding, maybe Larry Bird would have stayed. Sometimes, I think nothing would have stopped them. In later years, Coach Knight admitted that his handling of Bird was a big mistake.

In the end, this amazing man has been reduced to negative memories. It's ironic. The man who demanded such discipline had so little self-control. I'll admit that every time I share this bit on stage, I worry that the General will storm through the doors, carrying a baseball bat, and take me out! I do stand by the point: no jerks allowed. Even when they approach the Steve Jobs level of competence in their field, they often end up remembered for all the wrong reasons.

# Story 19

# Appreciating Failure: *They're Going to Boo Me Off the Stage*

So much of what we're capable of, we don't even attempt. The main reason is that we've been conditioned to fear failure and mistakes. Instead of a fun learning orientation, people adopt a negative risk avoidance orientation. Your choice between these two options determines a great deal about your success.

This is one of life's biggest ironies since a strong love of learning is the backbone of personal improvement and corporate innovation. No real improvement ever happens without lots of mistakes, missteps, half-baked ideas, failed attempts, and so on. Failure is always the first step toward success. Only when you know this and believe this do you find the strength to persevere through setbacks.

Maybe the most profound example I've run across involved a man who wanted to be a politician. He failed in business in 1831. He ran for the state legislature and lost in 1832. He tried business again in 1833 and failed again. His sweetheart died in 1835. He suffered a nervous breakdown in 1836. He was defeated in a run for Congress in 1843 and defeated again for Congress in 1848. He was defeated once more when he ran for the Senate in 1855, defeated when he ran for the vice presidency of the United States in 1856, and defeated for a run at the Senate again in 1858. Thankfully, he never gave up, and in 1860, Abraham Lincoln became the sixteenth president of the United States. That's perseverance.

I have endured quite a few screw-ups and failures thus far in life. Slowly but surely, I realized I could learn something useful each time. Eventually, this process changed my life. I went from fear of failure to fear of not trying. Over the years, I realized that we have to make a decision. When we are elderly and reminiscing about life, we can look back with pride at the risks we avoided, happy to have not suffered major catastrophes. Or we can look back and take pride in the fact that, win or lose, we truly lived. We remember the failures, but most important, we remember how they helped us realize some of our biggest dreams. What's your choice?

To get you thinking about some of your most stupendous mistakes, I'll share a few of mine. You have to learn to openly talk about them, own them, and even laugh about them. That's when fear starts to shift toward learning.

I could tell you about the time at age sixteen when I was fired from my job at the local frozen yogurt store. Apparently, giving away free yogurt to your friends isn't smart, even if you know that everyone else is doing it.

I could tell you about the time I wrote not one, but two novels. The creative process was exhilarating. The final product was embarrassing. Maybe even unreadable.

Instead of those or other stories, I thought I'd share the story of my most embarrassing moment. It involves something sacred to me: speaking. It's like Ralph Waldo Emerson said, "All great speakers were bad speakers at first." Don't I know it.

A few years after I began speaking professionally, I received a call from a meeting planner at State Farm Insurance. A manager at State Farm found my website and read my latest book. They wanted me to speak to a regional conference of State Farm managers. I checked the dates to see if I was available. We negotiated the fee. It was a done deal. Yes!

What they did not know was that they had just booked me for my very first big-time keynote address. Up until that point, I was speaking for hundreds of bucks per gig. They wanted to pay me several thousand. I couldn't believe it. I viewed this as undeniable evidence that I was breaking through to another level. I was amped and ready to go. *Look out, world! Dr. Dewett the keynote master has finally arrived!*

Before the event, I had been more of a trainer/workshop guy, not a real speaker. I told stories, but they were not highly polished. Nonetheless, I'm energetic and funny, and the audience always laughed and learned. I assumed this gig would be no different. I was dead wrong.

I looked around the room while a State Farm executive was on stage reading my introduction. Several hundred ambitious and well-educated middle managers sat, waiting for me. They wanted to be entertained and educated. They wanted a show—a real, live keynote worth remembering!

They didn't get it.

After the introduction, I took the stage to polite applause. Keep in mind, I read nonverbal behavior very well. I launched into a quick hello and more about my background (moron move for a speaker) and slowly but surely began to deliver a few rough stories. I saw it within minutes. The smiles faded. The enthusiasm evaporated. The audience was not appalled, but boy oh boy, they were not fans. Ten minutes in, the looks of disinterest and boredom were painfully clear. I honestly thought they might boo me off the stage. Thankfully, they were respectful.

For just a moment, I thought, *Why don't they react like the other audiences I've seen?* Slowly, it dawned on me that a workshop with a small number of people was considerably different than a keynote on stage in front of many people. The most painful part of the actual event was that I recognized their disinterest very early in the presentation, but I had no idea at all what to do about it. I continued the best I knew how. They continued to not care. I'd never before seen so many people e-mailing and texting on their phones. It was like I was talking to myself.

When I was done about an hour later, I received the most insincere and brief applause you can imagine. The audience was just happy it was over and wanted to move on to happy hour. I felt like an idiot. I left the stage and approached my table, where everyone was now standing since the event was over. The executives smiled fake smiles and thanked me. One of them handed me a check for several thousand dollars. This was the only time in my career that I felt guilty for taking the fee. I was sweaty and shaken. I just wanted to get out of the building.

The gig was in a major city not far from where I lived in the Midwest, so I drove instead of flying. That drive home was the most difficult three hours I'd ever spent in a car. Normally, I am overflowing with confidence. Not that day. I felt like a moron who thought he was good at something but apparently was too full of himself to know that he was just mediocre.

I was sitting on what my mother used to call the pity pot. That's a mental place you go when you want to feel sorry for yourself and wallow in thoughts about your horrible lot in life. My mother gave me some beautiful advice about the pity pot. She said that it's a universal experience. We all go there now and again. The trick to overcoming the unproductive pity pot is to recognize that it is real, that you're sitting on it, that you need to make the choice to stand up, and that you're going to give yourself a very real timeline to do just that.

I had developed the habit of never allowing more than a day or two on the pity pot. After that much time down in the dumps, I would decide to shake it off, take a deep breath, consciously choose a positive perspective, and move on productively. Sometimes, this little mental process can be difficult, but it really does help.

After only a couple hours on that drive home, I mentally removed myself from the pity pot. When I did, I realized something. That ridiculously mediocre talk I delivered could be the end of my fledgling attempts to be a professional speaker or the beginning of the time when I really started to improve. I thought for only a few minutes before choosing to make it a new beginning.

When I made that choice, the next steps became clear. I began breaking down what I had done in my mind, mentally watching myself on stage in front of the State Farm crowd. I quickly identified several things I had done wrong. Things I had to change. Some elements I had to add. Others I had to remove. Then, I realized that I was blessed to live in the era of YouTube!

I returned home, jumped on the Net, and began watching videos of many of the greatest speakers of all time: politicians, businesspeople, preachers, motivational speakers, sports figures, and so on. I took extensive notes. I identified discrete ways I could start improving what I was doing as a performer by stealing from the greats.

Slowly but surely over the next year, gig after gig, I began experimenting while in front of audiences. I would actively work on only one variable per gig. It might be pacing, the use of pauses, or a particular type of movement. A new me began to emerge. I finally gained an ability to think about what I was doing while I was actually speaking instead of only being able to reflect afterward. As a result, I started to figure out what a keynote could be for the first time.

Today, keynoting represents the vast majority of my speaking engagements. While it's true that every performer has some variance in their delivery, on average, I'm nailing it these days. Every gig, people laugh, learn, and cry. The polite applause has grown into something significantly more enthusiastic, including the occasional standing ovation.

Why? Because the nice folks at State Farm were kind enough to endure me that day so many years ago. The show-your-ink lesson here is to choose learning over self-pity. After a short spell on the pity pot, I recognized an opportunity and chose to grow. I realized that you move forward faster when you confront your mistakes and use them. Short-term pain, long-term gain. Are you ready to move forward faster?

(Dear State Farm: If you guys ever call me again, you will receive a ridiculous discount.)

# Story 20
# Finding Creative Answers:
## *Order the Combo Platter*

As a leader, sometimes you have to realize that even when you're right, you can be wrong in the eyes of others. You see a path that will work, and you make the decision and tell the team to follow you. You often assume it's the only path. Further, you assume others should accept the decision and be happy with it. What we sometimes fail to remember is that there is always more than one way to skin a cat. When we latch on to one allegedly correct course of action, our conviction can blind us from seeing other creative possibilities—possibilities that others on the team might like better than the one you chose.

This was one of the many lessons Dad taught me. He was the kind of man who took pride in the fact that his undershorts had a few stains in them. He loved that his undershorts had a few holes in them too. To put it bluntly, his tighty-whities were no longer tight or white.

Both men and women are guilty of this, but we all know men are far worse. They love to hold on to underwear that no longer holds on to them.

I was walking through the den one day when I was thirteen years old, and I saw my father folding laundry. He pulled a pair of wrecked and tattered drawers out of the basket. I stopped, shook my head, and said, "Dad, why do you keep those things? I don't even think they can be classified as underwear anymore."

He didn't miss a beat. He said, "Maybe, but they keep your mother away from me."

We both laughed at his crude joke. In truth, he loved those old drawers for the same reason he loved the duct tape holding together the front seat of his car. It was the same reason he celebrated after having worn a hole through the bottom of his shoe. These things were reminders of how great my dad was at stretching a dollar. He was the master of being frugal. At times, he was just plain cheap. He was spectacular at managing our very small family budget, and he took great pride in that ability.

I loved that he was so responsible with his pennies, but here's the problem. He was a kooky zealot at times. He felt that the rest of the family should follow his lead. If he could wear his shoes until they fell apart, we should too. If he could wear off-brand clothes from Goodwill until they were threadbare, well, so should we.

The problem with this plan was my mother.

Unlike my dad, she was a normal person when it came to money. She was always reasonable about our financial reality and never asked for much, but every couple years she wanted a few new simple pieces of clothing from Sears or JCPenney—not Goodwill! Every time she spoke up, usually around her birthday, Dad would throw a fit and scream about our tiny budget. He almost always got his way.

I watched this act play out time and again, and it bothered me. Aside from the fact that it reinforced how little money we had, it made me feel sad for both of my parents. I thought Dad was right to be a miser with the little money we had. I thought Mom was right because her request was small and simple and deserved. Mostly, I was just mad. I was a young teenager and knew I couldn't have the designer jeans and Nike tennis shoes I wanted.

The dynamic wasn't any different when Dad wanted to spend money. In the spring, when the lawn-mower died and seemed beyond repair, he announced that he would be purchasing a new one. Mom protested immediately—"How come you're allowed a new mower, but everything else around here has to be secondhand?" Dad ended that spat as he always did, by raising his voice and making some nonsensical proclamation. This time, he said, "The grass has to get cut, Judy! I'm buying a mower." Dad did his research, waited for a sale, and bought a cheap new lawnmower.

Not long after, Mom's birthday rolled around. That afternoon after Dad finished mowing the lawn with his shiny new mower, he came inside where my mom, my brother, and I were sitting in the den, watching television. We knew what was coming.

Three or four times each year, we'd go as a family to a restaurant for dinner to celebrate one of our birthdays. There was only one type of restaurant my father would allow us to visit: a buffet. You pay one flat price per person, and you can stuff yourself until you pop. You have no idea how much money those establishments lost on my father. He had a bottomless stomach and no shame. It was embarrassing. Long after the rest of us had given up, he kept shoveling. When Dad would announce that the family was going out for dinner, my mother would sometimes politely suggest a trip to Red Lobster—"a real restaurant," she would add under her breath. Dad would scoff and take us to the buffet.

That day, he walked in and announced, "Folks, it's your mother's birthday, and we're going out for dinner tonight. Everyone get cleaned up!" Mom didn't even ask where we were going. She had acquiesced to his ways. *Bring on the buffet,* she figured. After cleaning up, we piled in our old red station wagon with the saggy ceiling.

Todd Dewett Ph.D.

A few minutes later when my dad made an unex-pected turn in traffic, Mom spoke up. "Charlie, where are you going? Isn't the buffet that way?"

"It's your birthday," he said, "and we're going to Red Lobster."

His reply shocked her. Mom gasped and then grinned like a schoolgirl. My brother and I were thrilled too because at Red Lobster, we could drink Shirley Temples and feel like adults sipping cocktails.

Watching my father read the menu was absolutely hilarious because we all knew he was dreaming of a buf-fet crammed with every last thing he was reading about. When the waitress arrived, she took Mom's order, my brother's order, and then mine. Finally, she said to my father, "Sir, what can I get you?"

He said, "Fisherman's Platter, please." Eureka! Well played, Dad. For his dear wife, he passed on the buffet restaurant, but he did order the biggest combo plate at Red Lobster. It included fried shrimp, scallops, crab, hush puppies, and more. Not in the quantities Dad wanted, but pretty darn good anyway.

Mom beamed as she ate her birthday meal with her family.

On the drive home, for the second time, Dad made another unexpected turn.

Surprised, Mom spoke up. "Charlie, where are we going now?"

"Macy's," he replied. "About time you had a new blouse, isn't it? Let's go find one."

Her jaw dropped. Quietly, she said to him, "We don't have to spend that kind of money, babe."

He replied, "It's OK. You know that three hundred dollars I saved up for the mower? I actually went in with Ray next door so we could both save a buck. The rest of the money was for your birthday."

My mom looked like she was about to cry. She kissed him on the cheek and then wrapped her arm in his for the remainder of the drive to the mall. She was thoroughly enjoying her birthday.

In the backseat, my brother piped up. "The mall? Can we get new Nikes, Dad? Please!"

At the same time, Mom and Dad said, "No!"

Like many managers I've come to know over the years, my dad was a bit of a hardhead. It took him a while to see that there might be multiple paths to each goal—and that some of them might allow for a little wiggle room with which to get creative. My dad, the cheapskate, had learned how to cleverly loosen up just a bit in order to make the budget work while also making room to give a much-deserved thank-you to my mother.

Twenty-five years later, I was holding Dad's hand while he lay in bed during the last few weeks of his battle with cancer. We were laughing. We were laughing because we were reminiscing about funny things we could remember throughout life. Silly things we had all done at some point in the past.

At one point, I said, "Dad, do you remember that time when I was a teenager and I stopped in the den to laugh at you and your ridiculously worn-out old drawers?"

He said, "You're damn right I do. I'm wearin' 'em right now."

We laughed until we cried.

Sometimes, it's hard for old dogs to learn new tricks. Other times, they might surprise you by ordering the combo platter instead of going to the buffet.

Goal attainment is spectacular, but ultimately, it's hollow if the team is too worn-out or feels too neglected. Strive to find solutions that meet your needs while also allowing you to support and reward the team. In the end, his shortcomings aside, my dad was a pretty good leader for our family. Years from now, what will your team say about you?

# Closing

When I wrote these stories, I had a few very specific themes in mind. As I noted in the introduction, things expanded over time. Nonetheless, the stories represent various core rules in life that are dear to me. They can be useful to anyone who wishes to be more successful and fulfilled.

I recognize that what you might take away from the stories will differ from what I intended. Any time we hear a song, watch a movie or a play, hear a speech, or read a book, they speak to us uniquely. Where I saw sacrifice, discipline, goal setting, and humility, you no doubt saw many additional themes. That's fine with me. Take from them what speaks to you.

More important, I want to ask two things of you.

First, strive to find your own useful stories. As a leader, a colleague, a friend, or a parent, you too will find opportunities to help others through stories. We all have them. They are the lessons we learn at every stage of life. If you spend a few minutes thinking about it, I'm sure you'll think of a few worth sharing. Then, simply remain alert for the right time to share them. When a person is troubled, sometimes the helpful response is listening. Other times, it is teaching. When you teach, try to resist dictating and preaching. Instead, remember the power of a simple story.

Second, if you're going to be a decent teacher to those around you, it's incumbent on you to model continuous improvement. So here is the call to action: browse the stories once more. Identify one or two actionable items that you can begin to apply to yourself. For many of us, it's easiest to start small, gain a nice win, and then build momentum. How will you apply the one or two lessons that you enjoyed the most in order to become a better professional and a better person? Make a specific behavioral plan. Be concise. It should only require a few sentences. Share it with a close friend or mentor who will help hold you accountable. That's it. You're now on your way to becoming a better version of yourself.

Good luck to you. Thanks for reading my stories.

61547719R00103

Made in the USA
Lexington, KY
13 March 2017